MW01064829

SPEAKING
FAITH-FILLED
WORDS

HOW WORDS SHAPE YOUR WORLD

DR. ED KING

Parsons Publishing House
Melbourne, Florida USA

Speaking Faith-Filled Words—How Words Shape Your World
by Ed King

Parsons Publishing House
P. O. Box 410063
Melbourne, FL 32940 USA
www.ParsonsPublishingHouse.com
Info@ParsonsPublishingHouse.com

All Scripture quotations, unless otherwise indicated, are taken from the Holy Bible, King James Version, Cambridge, 1769. Public Domain. All rights reserved. Scripture quotations marked (CEV) are from the Contemporary English Version Copyright © 1991, 1992, 1995 by American Bible Society, Used by Permission. Scripture quotations marked (AMPC) are taken from The Amplified® Bible Classic Edition. Copyright © 1954, 1958, 1962, 1964, 1965, 1987 by The Lockman Foundation. Used by permission. Scripture quotations marked (TLB) are taken from The Living Bible copyright © 1971. Used by permission of Tyndale House Publishers, Inc., Carol Stream, Illinois 60188. All rights reserved. Scripture quotations marked (NIV) are taken from the Holy Bible, New International Version®, NIV®. Copyright © 1973, 1978, 1984 by Biblica, Inc. TM Used by permission of Zondervan. All rights reserved worldwide. www.zondervan.com. Scripture quotations marked (GW) are taken from GOD'S WORD®. Copyright © 1995, 2003, 2013, 2014, 2019, 2020 by God's Word to the Nations Mission Society. Used by permission. Scripture quotations marked (NLT) are taken from the Holy Bible, New Living Translation, copyright 1996. Used by permission of Tyndale House Publishers, Inc., Wheaton, Illinois 60189. All rights reserved. Scripture quotations taken from the (NASB®) New American Standard Bible®, Copyright © 1960, 1971, 1977, 1995, 2020 by The Lockman Foundation. Used by permission. All rights reserved. lockman.org. Scripture quotations marked (CEB) are taken from the Common English Bible. © Copyright 2011 Common English Bible. All rights reserved.

This book or parts thereof may not be reproduced in any form, stored in a retrieval system, or transmitted in any form by any means—electronic, mechanical, photocopy, recording or otherwise—without prior written permission of the publisher, except as provided by the United States copyright law.

Copyright © 2023 by Ed King.
All rights reserved.
ISBN-13: 978-160273-148-6
ISBN-10: 160273148-9
Library of Congress Control Number: 2023932095
Printed in the United States of America.
For World-Wide Distribution.

TABLE OF CONTENTS

1

Enjoying Life

It is exciting to talk about the power of speaking faith-filled words and how using the right words goes a long way toward allowing you to enjoy life.

When the Bible talks about your lips, many times, it is referring to your physical lips, but it's not just referring to your lips as a place to layer lipstick. It is talking about what flows through them—what you speak. God has a lot to say about it. There are multitudes of Scripture that talk about the power of your tongue and how much control it has over your life.

Without much reservation, we could say that most of what we do in life is done to help us live a better life, whether it is the pursuit of jobs, careers, family, home, or hobbies—all the things consuming our time and money. We all want to improve and have a good life, and for parents, it is often to help our children live better lives than we have ever known. So, we spend a great deal of our time, energy, and substance trying to find a way to have a better life.

> "For he that will love life, and see good days, let him refrain his tongue from evil, and his lips that they speak no guile" (1 Peter 3:10).

This Scripture shows us a way—but not the only one—that is foundational to all the other ways of having a good life. It says, "For he that will love life." We could translate the word "love" as *enjoy*. In fact, it's translated that way in a number of different versions. Plugging that word into the verse, it says, *"For he that will enjoy life."* God wants you to enjoy life.

Often, people have this religious notion that sacrifice is holy, but it's not necessarily etched in stone. Sacrifice might be holy under the right set of circumstances. For example, if God asks you to sacrifice something, it could be a sacred thing. But the Bible says obedience is greater than sacrifice; to obey the Lord is more excellent than sacrifice. God did not put you on this planet trying to torture you and make things difficult. Instead, God gave us abundant life through Jesus.

> The thief cometh not, but for to steal, and to kill, and to destroy: I am come that they might have life, and that they might have it more abundantly (John 10:10).

The Bible says that God wants you to enjoy life. Some versions translate this verse as Jesus came to give us life so that we may enjoy it fully until it overflows. Let's look at the Amplified version:

> The thief comes only in order to steal and kill and destroy. I came that they may have and enjoy life, and have it in abundance (to the full, till it overflows) (John 10:10, AMPC).

God wants you to enjoy your life. However, that doesn't mean you should live a life full of frivolous nonsense. It does not mean that all we do is listen to comedians and watch YouTube® the entire day, experiencing unabated silliness and hilarity.

You must take life seriously and be sober-minded concerning it. God wanted to put you on this earth to experience a journey—eventually running headlong into His presence—where you stand before Him and hear, "Well done, good and faithful servant." Beyond that, He wants you to enjoy the trip. However, many times, we become so destination-oriented that we miss everything the journey has to offer.

We don't realize that God has a plan for us to enjoy the entire experience. God wants you to enjoy the journey as well as end up at the right place. He certainly wants you to settle in your heart where the destination is for your life. Our Heavenly Father wants you to be ready to stand before Him one day, and we do that by coming through the blood of His Son, Jesus Christ. He wants you to be prepared for that, but He wants you to enjoy the trip. However, there is a process that we need to go through.

Some time back, I was talking to Mylon LeFevre, the Christian singer and preacher, and he told me, "Ed, if you're not enjoying life, you're doing it wrong." Profound thought.

God wants you to enjoy your life. He put you here to have joy in this place, not to be tormented and worried every time you turn on the news. He doesn't want you wringing your hands and dealing with an elevated heart rate every day. God did not put you here for that.

Earlier, we looked at 1 Peter 3:10, which says, "For he that would love or enjoy life and see good days, let him refrain his tongue..." Every single person I know wants a life they can enjoy and be full of good days. Everyone is out here trying to get it, trying to buy it—just trying to find a way to have it. That is what everyone is after—having an enjoyable life with good days in the process.

Refrain Your Tongue from Evil

Your tongue has a lot to do with your power to enjoy life and your ability to see good days. Scripture says, let him refrain his tongue from evil and his lips that they speak no guile—or deceit. The Amplified Bible says it this way:

> "For let him who wants to enjoy life and see good days [good—whether apparent or not] keep his tongue..." (1 Peter 3:10, AMPC).

Sometimes you may think it's a bad day when it's actually a good day. God turns what is terrible and makes it favorable. The final judge has yet to issue the ruling. It may look bad now, but you don't know where that bad thing may lead. Maybe you received a pink slip—a job-loss notice—or you are losing this or losing that. But let me just say that the final word is not in yet. God has a plan and a purpose for you.

Even amidst bad and unwelcome news, the Bible says to refrain your tongue from evil, talking about the downside of it. Instead, start talking about the upside and the victory. Talk about the plan of God. Remind God that you are in His hands. Start speaking your deliverance now.

A person could respond by saying, *"But I think it's enough to **think** good thoughts if I want good days."* Wrong. It is not enough just to keep your thoughts in line with the Bible; you must also control what you speak. We must refrain our tongues from evil to enjoy life.

SPEAKING FAITH-FILLED WORDS

2

SATISFIED LIVING

> A man's belly shall be satisfied with the fruit of
> his mouth; and with the increase of his lips shall
> he be filled. Death and life are in the power of
> the tongue: and they that love it shall eat the
> fruit thereof (Proverbs 18:20-21).

Let's walk through this passage. Do you know what a man's "belly" refers to in the Bible? It is not that thing hanging over your belt. A man's belly is his inner man—the core of his being. John 7:38 says, "He that believeth on me, as the scripture hath said, out of his belly shall flow rivers of living water." God's Word says that from out of your belly—out of the inside of you—shall flow rivers of living water. Your belly is your innermost being. When Scripture refers to your heart, it's not talking about the organ that pumps blood; it means the core of who you are. So, out of the core of who you are—your belly—shall flow rivers of living water.

You do not necessarily have to have everything exciting and happy around you to enjoy internal satisfaction. There is a lot of evil on this earth, but you can be at peace while all hell is going on around you. You can have a little bit of heaven in the middle of the torment and anguish of a hellish situation.

Proverbs 18:20 says, "A man's belly shall be satisfied with the fruit of his mouth." To be "satisfied" is being content, fulfilled, or satiated. It paints an image of being satisfied to the full until it overflows. When you fill a glass with water until it runs down the outside, it is filled, satisfied, quenched, or satiated. If you drop a sponge in a pail of water for a few minutes, it will soak up an enormous amount of liquid. It gets so soppy wet that when you pick it up, it drips everywhere. That is a description of being satiated; it means satisfied. God wants you to be so satisfied with your life that His presence drips from you. That is what He wants for you.

Let's expand this verse a bit:

> "A man's belly shall be satisfied with the fruit of his mouth; and with the increase of his lips shall he be filled" (Proverbs 18:20).

When you start talking the blues and start crying, moaning, and groaning, you are going to lose your satisfaction, inner peace, and the joy God put in you. That ability to enjoy life is going to leave you. God wants you to be satisfied with life. He does not want you to turn into a complainer, whiner, or griper. Every time you get into self-pity, you are going to lose the joy of the Lord.

I hear people say, *"Oh, woe is me. What am I going to do?"* Let me help you with that. You might have received some unwelcome news, but it's not "woe is me;" it's woe on the devil because he is under my feet. Let your faith do some talking. Do you remember that old Yellow Pages® commercial several years ago with the line, "Let your fingers do the walking?" Well, in this case, let your faith do the talking! If your fingers can do the walking, your faith can do some talking.

Take a look at Proverbs 18:20b, which says, "and with the increase of his lips shall he be filled." This verse does not say the "decrease of his lips." That's a significant difference. In the middle of a financial downturn, when your 401(k) is poised to **lose** value, we need to talk about an **increase** instead. We must fight back, not lie down and take it. It's time to use our faith. Do something about it! We need to be satiated, overflowing, pouring out, and dripping with the presence of God.

Proverbs 18:21 goes on to say, "Death and life are in the power of the tongue: and **they that love it** shall eat the fruit thereof" (emphasis, added). This truth is serious stuff that God said can kill you or give you life. So, if a man loves life and wants to see good days—if you want to enjoy the life you have—then control the words that come out of your mouth.

Where are death and life controlled? The answer is: in the power of the tongue. This verse says that if you love "it." What is "it" in this verse—life or the tongue? The answer is the tongue. In other words, what comes out of your mouth. For those who love the tongue, respect the tongue, honor the tongue, reverence the tongue, pay attention to the tongue, they shall eat the fruit of the tongue. People need to stop teaching religious things about this, saying, *"Well, that doesn't matter. I see, you're one of those faith people who name it and claim it."* No, I am one of those faith people who named it according to Scripture, claimed it according to the Bible, and got it in Jesus' name! There is a significant difference.

God says that you are planting a garden with your mouth. You are planting a garden with the words you speak. *"Oh, my back's killing me."* No, I don't think so. I could have said that recently. I've had a challenge with my back, but I told my back what it had to do according to the Word. Don't ask your back what it's going to do; you tell it what to do. I'm not just saying this; this is an absolute necessity that I live by. If you want to have a good life and you want to see good days, you must control the words of your mouth.

Remember, we are talking about speaking faith-filled words and the power and authority they produce. Words bring us satisfaction, and they bring us increase. They also can take us into life or death. Our words are critical to our future. Your future will never grow brighter than the words in your mouth. You will never be able to receive more than your words say you can receive.

The Bit—Our Tongue

> For in many things we offend all. If any man offend not in word, the same is a perfect [or mature] man, and able also to bridle the whole body (James 3:2, emphasis added).

This verse refers to the words of your mouth. "Perfect" translated here is a little misleading. None of us are perfect as far as being sinless and flawless. However, the word "perfect" in this context means *mature*.

You can bridle your body. That's what I'm talking about when I say: Don't ask your back what it's going to do; you tell it what it's going to do. This is the method you use to break every bad habit you are trying to break—every addiction or anything trying to beset you. That is how the process starts.

Some might say, *"Well, I said it once, and it didn't happen."* Let me help you get this straight. You probably have been confessing negative and unwise things every day of your life. Now you say something to the contrary—something positive and scriptural—and expect a lifetime of misspent declarations to evaporate instantaneously. At least give your words of faith equal time. Start by letting the supernatural work for you instead of against you. To do that, we must talk in a certain way. This verse goes on to say:

> "Behold, we put bits in the horses' mouths, that they
> may obey us; and we turn about their whole body"
> (James 3:3).

I've never been much of an equestrian—someone who rides and interacts with horses on a regular basis—but I know a little about them from some riding. I've found that if you pull the horse's reins in a particular direction, they are trained to go the way you tell them. Those reins are hooked to a small metal bit in their mouth that directs that big horse—which could do about anything it wanted to do—to obey the whims of the rider. The horse knows that it brings pain if they don't comply; they are trained to respond to the rider.

The Bible says your tongue is like a bit in a horse's mouth. It will guide your life; your tongue will take you where you want to go. It does not just happen; you make it happen.

A Ship's Rudder

Let's look at another translation of the following verse:

> Likewise, look at the ships: though they are so great and are driven by rough winds, they are steered by a very small rudder wherever the impulse of the helmsman determines (James 3:4, AMPC).

Have you ever been on a big ship? I'm not talking about a fishing boat of some kind, but a big ship—a battleship, aircraft carrier, or cruise ship? Some are as long as two or three football fields and crazy wide, too. These big supertankers and aircraft carriers are huge. But, as big as they are, if you could pick them up out of the water, you would see a little bitty thing on the back—maybe a couple of them—called a rudder. Those rudders move in the water a certain way, and they will turn and steer that gigantic ship. You can't steer a big ship with a bomb, but that little rudder can do it.

Just as that rudder does its job, the Bible says your life is that way. You have a rudder for your life called a tongue which are the words of your mouth. If you use your words properly under God's leadership, you can guide and direct the future of your life.

Do Something

God is sovereign, and He still has the power to give you direction. Please note: **You cannot confess things into your life that are contrary to His will for you and get Him to bless and honor them.** However, God gives you flexibility on many things. For example, how much money do you want to make? *"Well, God might get mad at me if I make too much."* The truth is that He might get upset with you if you make too little. If you're living below what He created you to be, it's not His will.

Life is a gift from God, but what you do with your life is your gift back to Him. Some people take life as it comes because they think it's just luck or because the cards have already been dealt. Let me tell you something; there are passels of things you didn't choose about life. You didn't choose your parents, skin color, IQ, talents, and many other things. Beyond that, there are a lot of choices that you make. When you take what God has given you, cultivating and using it for His glory to accomplish things, that's your gift back to Him.

God's not mad at you for achievement. In reality, He would be more upset with you for the lack of it. So, let's get out there and go for it. Do something. Take a shot!

One might ask, *"What if I fail?"* Well, what if you don't? I guarantee you that not trying—or attempting anything—is a failure on its own merits.

SPEAKING FAITH-FILLED WORDS

3

5 Things Words Will Do for You

Jesus gives us some instructions that I'm sure are familiar to you. In Matthew 6:24, the Word says you cannot serve both God and mammon (money). He goes on to tell you about how He will provide for your clothing and food. Then, there's a little phrase in the next verse that says, "Therefore I say unto you, **Take no thought** for your life…" (Matthew 6:25). Verse 27 says, "Which of you by **taking thought**…" Then verse 28 says, "And **why take ye thought**…" Later in verse thirty-one, it says again, "Therefore **take no thought,** saying…" So, the passage here is about what you think.

It's crucial to speak faith-filled words. Since our thoughts are critical in controlling our words, here are five things the Bible says your words will do for you:

1) Your words help control your attitude.

Your attitude controls your thoughts. Your words control how you feel about things. If you want, you can get all worked up over nothing, or you can calm it down. You have the ability to lay it to the side if you so desire.

We built a house a couple of years ago, and we had a great builder. I have built homes before, and I know how it works. Builders can be gruff and yell at people because being loud gets attention. So, before we broke ground on this house, I had a conversation with the builder, and I told him, *"We're friends now, and we'll be friends when we're finished. Through this process, we will never have one argument."*

A person might say, *"I'll never build another house. That thing almost killed me."* Maybe it almost killed you because you didn't say what I said; it's not going to kill me. I determined my attitude about everything before I even started the process. Now, that doesn't mean everything went right in the building process; it doesn't mean everything was flawless. It does mean, however, that you make a decision about how you are going to react.

The Bible says to take no thought saying. There are a bazillion thoughts flying through the air right now, but you don't **take** any of those thoughts until you say them. They become yours—you possess them—when you speak them out. Just because you think something, it doesn't necessarily mean you own it; you only own it when you say it. Your words can and will control your attitude.

The minute something rises up out of your mouth from a fit of anger, everyone loses, especially you. Someone says, *"I'm just going to speak my mind."* Well, maybe you shouldn't. Perhaps you should be led instead of impulsively blurting something inappropriate out of your mouth. Stop, take a minute, and think about it; you will come out better.

Catch the Right Wave

Your words will control your attitude or how you feel about something. You can calm it down by saying, *"No! I don't allow that. Right now, in Jesus' name, I am not going to let this upset me."* That is a choice you make, and the minute you do it, everything just settles back down. The devil's trying to work you up. Your flesh is trying to work you up—make you irritated and agitated. Then, a little later, someone comes along and feeds it, telling you why you should be worked up and why you need to be agitated. When that happens, you must put it down again.

This passage in Matthew has God saying to us, "Take no thought... Take no thought... Why take ye thought?" We take thoughts by **saying** them. Thoughts come and go, but you possess them as your own when you speak them out.

In my office, there are all kinds of waves traveling through it. There are TV and radio waves in the air. There are also WIFI and Bluetooth signals. If you have the right equipment, you can "catch the wave."

The air is full of waves and signals—they are everywhere. It's your choice which signal you are going to receive—from God, your flesh, a friend, or the devil. So, reach out and catch a good one; it's much better for you than grabbing a bad one.

2) Your words create an atmosphere around you.

Your words charge the atmosphere and create an environment immediately around you.

Do you remember the story of the 12 spies that went into the Promised Land? Ten spies returned with bad news; the Bible calls it an evil report. Scripture says in Psalm 34:13 to refrain your tongue from evil and your lips from speaking guile. These spies returned with an evil report of inability and unbelief, saying, *"We can't do this. There are giants in the land, and we are as grasshoppers in our own sight."* They reported that it couldn't be done.

Twelve spies came back, but only Joshua and Caleb said, *"Let's go up at once because we are well able to overcome them."* It took forty years, but they eventually walked into the Promised Land. They possessed what they said.

The ten spies sowed unbelief to the whole congregation:

> "And all the congregation lifted up their voice,
> and cried; and the people wept that night"
> (Numbers 14:1).

The crowd's reaction came about as a result of the evil report; they created this environment.

Your words create an environment. If you walk into a place where there has been a spat, fuss, quarrel, or maybe even worse, you can feel it. It begins to oppress the room. Alternatively, if you go into a room where people have been rejoicing and are happy, you can feel that, too. Words create atmospheres, and the air becomes charged with a negative or positive quality. Words do that.

You can fill the air with faith or unbelief. For instance, you talk about overcoming, or you can go on and on about how you are going under. Words create your attitude and can possibly create the attitude of those around you— but they must make some decisions, too.

When Ronald Reagan was president, he always had the ability to instill and inspire hope in the American people. That's why he will go down in history as one of the great presidents. In the midst of trouble, difficulty, and economic downtimes, he said to the American people, *"This is a tough time we are in now, but we're going to make it."* You have no idea what a leader can do with their words. A leader must be able to give hope to people.

The less-than-stellar economic situations we see from time to time are nothing but people being unwilling to spend because fear has been charging the atmosphere. At times like this, our leaders need to stand up, take charge, and give hope to the people of this nation. That's how we should pray for our president and others.

3) He shall have whatsoever he sayeth.

> For verily I say unto you, That whosoever shall say unto this mountain, Be thou removed, and be thou cast into the sea; and shall not doubt in his heart, but shall believe that those things which he saith shall come to pass; he shall have whatsoever he saith (Mark 11:23).

Does this verse say that we shall have whatsoever we **thinketh**? Is that right? No. It actually says he shall have whatsoever he **sayeth**.

Let's look at that verse from a couple of different translations of the Bible:

In reply Jesus said to the disciples, "If you only have faith in God—this is the absolute truth—you can say to this Mount of Olives, 'Rise up and fall into the Mediterranean,' and your command will be obeyed. All that's required is that you really believe and have no doubt!" (Mark 11:22-23, TLB).

If you have faith in God and don't doubt, you can tell this mountain to get up and jump into the sea, and it will. Everything you ask for in prayer will be yours, if you only have faith (Mark 11:23-24, CEV).

4) Your words will release faith to assault your problems or troubles.

Your words release opposition to your problems and troubles. Those mountains are representative of life's challenges that you face. God said to speak to the mountain, and it will obey **you**; the Bible does not say it will obey God. If you are waiting on God to move a mountain, it will stand there and laugh at you because it will not move if you're waiting on God to move it. Therefore, it is imperative that **you** speak to it.

Without question, God must get involved, but He will only go where you say to go; He won't go unless you tell Him. He is the Apostle and High Priest of our profession. God becomes the High Priest, watching over your profession to perform it. He is not going to do for you what you are unwilling to ask Him to do or do yourself. When you speak, it is your faith talking. You need to speak seriously to that mountain. Talk to that pink slip or layoff notice. Talk to your bank account and retirement fund. You must talk back to it!

Someone says, *"Well, I heard that once before."* You may have heard it once before, but are you doing it? Things change not because of what you've heard; it's what you are doing with what you hear that changes things. Your words are your faith talking because God said to speak to the mountain.

> It's not only what you've heard; it's what you are doing with what you've heard.

We are told to *speak to* the mountain, but what we primarily want to do is *talk about* the mountain. We want to talk about our problems instead of speaking to them. We want to tell everyone what our problem is, how we can't make it, how we're going under, how we are never going to get ahead, and how everything's going bad. Sometimes we say things like, *"I don't know what we're going to do. Oh, Jesus, come on down!"* However, He's not here now. You must live out this thing called "life." He will get you out of here when the time is right; it could be soon, but that cannot be your alibi. You must live here. He put you here for a purpose, and He expects you to take dominion over the works of His hands.

> "Bless the Lord, ye his angels, that excel in strength,
> that do his commandments, hearkening unto the
> voice of his word" (Psalm 103:20).

The Bible says His Word has been sent forth into the earth; it's like the snow and rain that comes down. The Word has been sent into the earth, awaiting someone to give it voice. God's angels are standing at attention, waiting for His saints to give voice to His Word. **Your words, in cooperation and harmony with the words of the Bible, release angels to assist, help, and prepare a way for you.**

You cannot talk defeat and have victory. You cannot talk poverty and have prosperity. You cannot talk about things the news media tells you every day and see God move on your behalf. The Bible says that out of the abundance of the heart, the mouth speaks. So, when you watch the news in abundance, you begin to talk about it.

The difference between you and that television is that it has no power. But when you start speaking about the mess blaring at you, it starts gathering momentum. It may not have weight over everyone else, but it has weight over you. The Bible says:

> "For whatsoever is born of God overcometh the
> world: and this is the victory that overcometh the
> world, even our faith" (1 John 5:4).

This is the victory that overcomes the world, even our faith. You may not believe that it will overcome the entire world, but faith will certainly overcome in your world.

Your words give angels their assignment and tell them what to do. You say, *"They have already been sent out, doing what God tells them to do."* But God's not telling them what to do now; He told them to do what **you** say. That has already been declared. *"I don't believe that,"* you say. Well, you won't enjoy it, but it's the truth before God. The angels hearken unto the voice of the Word of God. In the Book of Genesis, you can read how He sent His angel before them to prosper the way (Genesis 24:40).

When you say words **in line with Scripture**, the angels are standing at attention, ready to go, do, make a way, and prepare.

5) Your words will create your future.

Look at this vitally important verse:

> My heart is inditing a good matter: I speak of the things which I have made touching the king: my tongue is the pen of a ready writer (Psalm 45:1).

Your tongue is the pen that writes your future. You may lament, *"I'll never make it. I'll go broke. We'll never get ahead."* I believe you should get a new pen and write something closer to the truth—the truth of God's Word. You must start saying what you want to happen. Don't just speak about the future you think somebody else wants you to have, but the future that God has put in your heart.

> ## You must begin to say what you want to have happen.

God has a dream for every person. He has a will that He wants to be manifested on this planet. Every individual has a God-given dream and a desire in their heart—something He wants that is consistent with His overall plan. I don't do what you do, nor do you do what I do. We don't copy one another. We are free agents under God to perform His will in the earth, and together, we form the Body of Christ that manifests His presence around the world. When we do that thing God put in us to do, we become contributors to this whole expression of the kingdom of God in the earth.

God has called some to make money. Some have been crafted by God with a creative bent—the ability to paint, draw, sing, or play an instrument—someone who has the power to express something. My part is preaching; that is what I'm called to do. What are you called to do?

Your words create your future. Your future is written by the words of your mouth. If we go back to the story of the twelve spies, ten of them reported back that they couldn't do it. They knew down deep that they were going to be overcome because the giants were great in the land. So, they were overthrown in the wilderness. Did you know the Bible says the Lord was not pleased with those who were overthrown in the wilderness? The Scripture says:

> "But with many of them God was not well
> pleased: for they were overthrown in the wilderness"
> (1 Corinthians 10:5).

The only ones who entered the Promised Land were Joshua, Caleb, and the children under twenty. They all got what they said. They wrote their future with the words of their mouth. Joshua and Caleb said they could go, and they did go into the Promised Land. Those who said they couldn't do it were overthrown in the wilderness.

Our confession should be: We can do it; we are going over. No grave or solemn news is greater than the God of the Bible. No power this earth can produce is greater than the covenant we have with Almighty God. None. We have a covenant with Almighty God, who said He would meet our needs according to His riches in glory by Christ Jesus, and so, therefore, that is the confession of my mouth.

Some might ask, *"Well, what are you going to do if the economy fails or that business closes?"* It doesn't change anything. The covenant is still intact; God is still on the throne, and I am still in His hands. All this stuff on earth is a temporary distraction that God will use. We have a covenant of increase, not decrease. I don't know how God's going to do it, but I'm going to increase. Even if everything around me is decreasing, I'm increasing. God will have to find another way to get it to me because I'm going to increase. That is my confession, and it should be yours, too.

SPEAKING FAITH-FILLED WORDS

4

WORDS THAT MOTIVATE

We currently live in a somewhat chaotic world inundated with an incredible amount of fear. As Christians, we must learn how to use our faith and participate in faith-inspired activities, even in the midst of uncertain times. God will use your faith—which is a gift from Him—to be your anchor. He will use that faith to dispel fear in you and take you into your future.

You can rest assured that what is going on in our society today is known to God. He is not somewhere far away, uninterested and unconcerned about what you are facing. In Psalm 138:8, God said He would perfect that which concerns you, and He is most certainly aware of those concerns. He has a plan and a purpose for you. God will turn the things we don't understand and shape them for good. I don't know how, but He will do it IF we use our faith, pray, and believe Him.

God's Plan to Use You

Let's look again at 1 Peter 3:10; it starts by saying, "For he that will love life…" It is vital for you to have a love for life. You may not love the circumstances that life has dealt you or the things that go on around you but having a love for life is a way we honor God. If you cannot be thankful for anything else, thank God that you are living above the grass and breathing. Life is a gift from God. What you do with that life is your gift back to Him.

However, you can't do what you can't do, and you can't be something you're not. You have a certain IQ, skin color, aptitude, personality, and gifting that God put within you. Your personality is all yours and no one else's. There are certain things that we were given that we did not ask for.

You may not like all the things you were given, but God put a package together when He made you. When He put you together, He put certain attributes and gifts inside you so they could take you into that dream He placed in you—your potential, your place, and your purpose—all things related to your life. God has given you a dream, and those giftings that He gave you are suited to that dream.

When you find God's dream for your life and understand that God has a purpose for you, all those gifts suddenly make sense. We are not to be envious of another's gifts because God has placed you here exactly as He wants you and will use you accordingly. He wants to use you not only for your benefit but for the benefit of others as well. I am somehow diminished, cheated, stolen from, and not all I need to be until I can enjoy **your** gifting. Your gifting was not only given to bless you; it was given to you to bless others.

God told Abraham, *"I want to bless you, and I want to make you a blessing. Through you shall all the families of the earth be blessed."* As Christians, we are of the faith of our father, Abraham, and the blessings of Abraham have come on us through Christ Jesus.

When God says, *"I want to use you to bless the families of the earth,"* you may not physically touch every family, but you will touch a good part of them because God wants you to do that. So, God put a gift in you so others could be blessed, which is marvelous. If we do not love life—the life that God has given us—we cheat others out of a great blessing. I want to receive what you have, and the Lord wants you to be able to give it out.

The Good Life

People are in pursuit of what they consider "the good life"—the enjoyment of life. Isn't that what the world is trying to do through hobbies, careers, entertainment of all kinds, alcohol, and illegal drugs? Alcohol, although not unlawful, is not the best for you. God is telling you that those things are not the ways of lasting enjoyment.

Let's look at that verse in 1 Peter in its entirety:

> "For he that will love life, and see good days, let him refrain his tongue from evil, and his lips that they speak no guile" (1 Peter 3:10).

He goes on in this verse to say—my translation: *"I have a way for you to see good days, and this is the way right here: your tongue speaks no evil, and your lips speak no guile."* God says the good life that He wants you to have begins with the words of your mouth. This is not the sum total of the whole, but it starts there. You can't speak bad things and have good. You can't speak wrong things and receive right. You can't speak evil and get good to come from it. You can't talk down and be up. You can't speak negatively and receive a positive outcome. God says your words are the beginning or entry point to living the good life.

People have a definition of the good life that differs from God's. It doesn't matter how much money you have because if you don't go to heaven or you don't have your health, you did not experience the good life. There is a lot more to the good life than just the stuff you've accumulated. God wants you to have the good life. If you're going to have the good life, it starts with the words of your mouth.

Let's look again in Proverbs:

> "A man's belly shall be satisfied with the fruit of his mouth; and with the increase of his lips shall he be filled" (Proverbs 18:20).

This verse is not just talking about eating a delicious meal. Your belly is your inner man. Another verse also speaks of our belly, "Out of [your] belly shall flow rivers of living water" (John 7:38, emphasis added).

The Bible says that your satisfaction in life—this deep inner satisfaction that He is talking about—can be experienced: "a man's belly shall be satisfied with the fruit of his mouth." God says if you are going to have that satisfied life that He wants you to have, it begins with the words—or fruit—of your mouth. So, your words are critical to living the good life; it all starts with what you say.

The verse immediately before this says, "A brother offended is harder to be won than a strong city: and their contentions are like the bars of a castle" (Proverbs 18:19). God draws a contrast here between contention and having a good life. If you stay in contention, you are going to have internal disharmony. To avoid this, He said you must get your mouth under control. Don't let controversy and struggles take the good life away from you.

Your Life is Like a House

When God talks about "the increase of [our] lips" in Proverbs 18, He is not just talking about monetary increase. Let's compare your life to a house. As you begin to build a house— as you start to say the right things—you begin to stack layer upon layer on top of the foundation: the subflooring, flooring, walls, roof, etc. You begin to build the kind of life God wants you to have and the kind of life that you should have. You increase by layering it line upon line, precept upon precept.

We begin with a confession that says, *"Thank God, Jesus is my Savior. I have made him the Lord of my life."* That is the entry point for the child of God—where we come in the door. On top of that, we discover that this house may have a lot of features that we don't know about, and we will not understand, never enjoy, and will never be able to receive them. For example, you must know how to turn on the television if you are going to watch it, and you need to know how to operate the HVAC system if you wish to remain comfortable year-round. You may have a whole-house stereo, but you need to know how to operate the system.

Your life is like that. There are many options that God has made available to us, but we will never know them unless we come into His Word. Only then will we begin to discover what is available to us from the Bible. So, first, we start putting His Word in our mouths and believing that we receive what He said about our lives. Then, we increase.

Where you come into this life of faith is not the end; it's the beginning. You increase from that entry point.

Confession Brings Deliverance

> "Death and life are in the power of the tongue:
> and they that love it shall eat the fruit thereof"
> (Proverbs 18:21).

This verse is not only talking about routine life on earth but about eternal life as well. The Bible says that if a man is to be born again, it is essential that he must believe in his heart and **confess with his mouth** that Jesus is Lord. The entry point into this whole thing called eternal life starts with your words. If you refuse to confess with your mouth or tell someone that Jesus is your Lord, it will never become real to you; it will never become a reality.

God said that if you are ashamed of Him and ashamed to confess Him before men, He will be ashamed to confess you before the Father in heaven. The New Living Translation says it this way:

> "Everyone who acknowledges me publicly here on
> earth, I will also acknowledge before my Father in
> heaven" (Matthew 10:32, NLT).

If we will not talk openly about our relationship with the Lord, we short-circuit our eternity If it works for eternal life, it will certainly work for our temporal lives because eternal life is more significant than temporal life. The things here on earth pass away; eternal things endure and last forever. So, the way into eternal life is partially, not totally, controlled by the words of our mouths. We must speak correctly.

In Proverbs 18:21, the Bible says there is fruit that comes from your words, and you can eat the fruit of those words. Scripture says if you talk about never making it, you will not make it. If you say, *"I can't get a job,"* you will not get one. Your confidence is controlled by the words of your mouth.

When you go for a job interview, what do you say? It all starts by looking in the mirror and talking to yourself. This should be your confession:

> *I'm a man (or woman) of God, full of the Holy Spirit. The Spirit of God lives inside me. My sufficiency is of God, and I am able because God is able. The Greater One lives in me, and He that is in me is greater than He that lives in the world. The place I'm going to apply for a job may not know it yet, but they need me. I can add benefit and value to them. They need me because I bring something to the table. I am not coming with my head down and my hat in hand; I am coming as a self-assured and confident man (or woman) of God. I am going in there boldly—but not arrogantly—because I will add value to them. They may not have*

discovered it yet, but they desperately need what
I can bring.

That kind of confession changes everything. You should never enter any business as a beggar; you should meet a potential employer humbly but with confidence in yourself. You don't want to go in arrogantly and push things around. Employers are looking for people who believe in themselves because if you don't believe in yourself, no one else will. You must believe you are capable because if you don't, you won't be.

I am not talking about bluffing. You may go into an arena where you are unfamiliar with their systems and how they operate, but your ability is of God. You have the mind of Christ and can learn whatever they put in front of you. It may be a new field for you, but you are capable. You are smart and intelligent, and God has gifted you. You can handle this.

Ramp up your confidence. The Bible says not to cast away your confidence, for it has great recompense of reward. So, you must turn up your confidence. Practice it before you go. Talk it up before you get there. Speak to yourself.

One may say, *"Well, they didn't hire me, and they put me down."* That has nothing to do with anything. They may be too ignorant to know what they need. You may have to go back again tomorrow and remind them. Do you see what I'm talking about? It is not over until you say it's over. *"We're not hiring,"* they say. Well, what has that got to do with anything? Your response could be: *"I wasn't looking for a job until today. You need to realize what an outstanding opportunity you have to get such a diamond and such a prize."*

Employers are looking for people with confidence. Again, I'm not talking about bluffing by being overconfident to the point that it's obnoxious. But people want employees with confidence. Businesses want people with a certain amount of boldness about them, and that's you; people can recognize the difference. However, you must produce once you get there, but all you need is a chance.

Once you turn on that confidence, people will begin to respond to you. It starts with the words of your mouth. That is where it all begins.

> For in many things we offend all. If any man offend not in word, the same is a perfect [or mature] man, and able also to bridle the whole body (James 3:2, emphasis added).

According to this verse, God said your maturity—or your perfection—is more controlled by the words of your mouth than any other thing, even more than your Bible knowledge or where you go to church. He said the condition, direction, and pursuits of your whole body are controlled by the words of your mouth.

Motivation Comes

Your activity or inactivity is also controlled by the words of your mouth. Have you ever had a motivation problem? Sure, you have; we all have at one time or another. There are some things that you would prefer not to do—yardwork quickly comes to mind. No one ever said, *"I just can't wait to get out there and pull some nasty weeds!"*

There are certain activities that you absolutely dread doing, but the Bible says that all motivation problems are controlled by the words of your mouth. So, if you have a motivation problem—something that is out there looming before you—the Bible says you can overcome all motivation problems by controlling the words of your mouth. Your body will respond to your words.

You can begin to tell yourself that it will not be as bad as you think. Get off the couch and mow that yard. You are going to have a ball mowing the yard today. Put your earbuds in and sing along! Nobody will hear you over the noise of the motor. What an opportunity to do something creative!

If the thought of exercising in any form gives you anxiety, you can change it. I refuse to tell myself that I don't like exercising. Instead, I remind myself that I love to exercise. I enjoy going to the gym; that's my escape. People ask me, *"How do you get motivated to keep in shape?"* I don't have to motivate myself; I love it. That's what I say all the time. For years, my confession has been: I love to go, and I do.

5

OVERCOMING OBSTACLES

> For in many things we offend all. If any man
> offend not in word, the same is a perfect man,
> and able also to bridle the whole body. Behold,
> we put bits in the horses' mouths, that they may
> obey us; and we turn about their whole body
> (James 3:2-3).

As we said earlier, a horse gets trained to respond to a little
metal bit in their mouth. For example, you can move a big 18-
hand horse—equal to six feet measured to the top of the
shoulder—by a little bit in his mouth. Certain bits cause
discomfort if the reins are pulled, so the horse obeys to keep
the pain at a minimum. The next thing you know, you have
control of the horse.

It is the same working principle as a ring in an enormous steer's
nose. They don't want that ring pulled because it hurts, so
they'll follow wherever it leads. If you pull on it, that big old
steer—which you cannot control otherwise—will obey you
because that nose ring motivates it to conform to your wishes.
So, God says your body and life are held fast by a ring called
your mouth.

That being said, if you don't like the life you have, you must change the words you are speaking. If you don't like the direction you are headed, you have to change what you say. There's more, but that is where it starts. If you want to turn something around, you must begin to say something different than what you've been saying. Begin speaking another way.

If you have said all your life, *"I'll never go to college; I'll never be smart enough; I'll never have enough money,"* you are right; you will never go. However, if you start by saying, *"I'm going to college because I'm smart enough, and I'll have the money to pay for it,"* you will be able to go. The longer you say it, the more power it has. If you don't like your life, it's crucial that you change what's coming out of your mouth!

You must understand that faith-filled words will overcome any obstacle. If you want to go to college, you need to say, *"Yes, I will go to college because I am more than smart enough, and I know how to apply myself. I am not distracted; I am single-minded. I can comprehend; I can think and discipline myself to study."* You can't say the opposite of that and get the results you want. If you don't stop that negative talk, you set in motion things that are going to hurt you.

Changes in the Spiritual Realm

You must go to some lengths to change your negative talk to positive. If you aspire to change who you are, you must alter your belief in yourself; you need to allow that new belief to come thundering from your mouth into the atmosphere and into the ears of all who can hear, including yours. Modifying the things you say will change where you are headed. That's how it starts—with that small but essential muscular organ in your mouth called your tongue—just like we control a horse with a bit, a steer with a nose ring, and a ship with a rudder. Small changes beget significant results.

The Living Bible goes on to say:

> "And a tiny rudder makes a huge ship turn
> wherever the pilot wants it to go, even though the
> winds are strong" (James 3:4, TLB).

If you're on the bridge of a ship where all the decisions take place, you don't have to walk to the stern and put your head underwater to see if the rudder is turned in the right direction. With the controls working properly, you can set the ship's course. If you can input the correct heading, that is precisely where the vessel is going.

From the bridge, you can turn a gigantic aircraft carrier by just knowing what lever to pull or button to push, and that action instigates the process. You don't have to understand how the rudder was manufactured, the inner workings of the hydraulics system, or the mechanisms that cause the rudders to move; that doesn't matter. All you need to know is what direction you want the bow of that ship to point.

God does not require us to know all the particulars. However, you must remember something about the faith realm: the unseen realm:

> "Faith is the substance of things hoped for, the
> evidence of things not seen" (Hebrews 11:1).

You are dealing with the realm of the spiritual world. That entire invisible world begins to respond to the words of your mouth. It begins to do that which you command.

Angels Respond

Angels, as we mentioned earlier, have much to do with your success or failure. In the book of Psalms, it says:

> Bless the Lord, ye his angels, that excel in strength, that do his commandments [His Word], hearkening unto the voice of his word (Psalm 103:20, emphasis added).

The Bible teaches that God's Word has been sent forth into the earth, and angels hearken to the voice of His Word. We see in Isaiah 55:11 where God's Word does not return to Him void. Think about it for a minute. God sent His Word ahead into the earth. How did He do this? In the form of a tennis ball? No, His Word returns to Him from the mouth of His children. The Lord says in Isaiah 43:26 to come and let us plead together—put Him in remembrance. So, we are to take God's Word and remind Him of what He said. You return His Word to Him in usable form. The Word profits us when mixed with the faith of those who hear it (Hebrews 4:2). Take His Word, pack it in a faith wrapper, send it back to Him, and tell Him what you want.

> For unto us was the gospel preached, as well as unto them: but the word preached did not profit them, not being mixed with faith in them that heard it (Hebrews 4:2).

40

In the case of Hebrews 4:2, the Word did not profit the Israelites because it was not mixed with faith. If His Word was in the earth without faith attached to it—faith that you must provide—it does no good. The Bible on your coffee table will not change anything. **It is the Word of God in your heart, springing from your mouth, that changes everything.** When you speak God's Word mixed with faith, the angels respond.

I want to give you a couple of crossover comparisons from 1 Peter and Ephesians.

> Unto whom it was revealed, that not unto themselves, but unto us they did minister the things, which are now reported unto you by them that have preached the gospel unto you with the Holy Ghost sent down from heaven; which things the angels desire to look into (1 Peter 1:12).

When the Word of God is preached, the angels come and listen to the sermons. I want you to think about that for a minute. In your church services, there are more angels than people present, and I do not doubt there are some outside the building, too. We know from the Bible that everyone has a guardian angel. Then the Bible mentions "the angel of the Church at Ephesus," so there must be an angel for the Church at Knoxville or the Church at Dallas. So, we know we have at least one more angel in church than we have people.

You deal in an invisible realm. So, whatever you say from God's Word, the angels hearken unto it. With that in mind, do you think sermons are important? I believe so. The sermons that are preached control the heavenlies and control the environment over a region. Why? Because the angels come and listen.

The reason angels come and listen is because many times, that is where they get their marching orders for what they need to do. If the churches are preaching unbelief, the angels don't have anything to do, but if the churches are preaching faith and victory, then the angels get to work.

You cannot preach negatively about the economy in a region and expect the angels to help improve it. You must speak favor and blessing over a region. You must release God's Word in it. You can't pronounce a curse over it; you must proclaim the blessing. You can't talk about how bad the economy is and expect it to get better. People need to say, *"We're going to make it."* Say it long and loud, and keep saying it over and over.

The United States is not great because of its inherent goodness or because it has resources. America's greatness is not because of its global positioning. Instead, America has been great because of the faith in the hearts of its people. If faith stays here, America will remain great.

If you cause people to believe in themselves, they will do remarkable things. If you encourage people and tell them they can do great things, they will step up and do it. If you tell them they are creative, they will be creative. If you tell them they are overcomers, they will overcome. If you tell them they are more than conquerors, they will conquer the "would-be" conquerors. We must do this because that's what the Bible says to do. We are not talking politics; we are talking faith. These things are essential because words bring hope.

Paul said, "I should preach among the Gentiles the unsearchable riches of Christ" (Ephesians 3:8). Paul is talking about preaching the riches, not the judgment. Speak hope!

The Mystery of the Gospel

Let's look more closely at Ephesians:

> Unto me, who am less than the least of all saints, is this grace given, that I should preach among the Gentiles the unsearchable riches of Christ; And to make all men see what is the fellowship of the mystery, which from the beginning of the world hath been hid in God, who created all things by Jesus Christ (Ephesians 3:8-9).

Do you know what the fellowship of the mystery of the Gospel is? The Bible says that if the princes of this world (the devil and his emissaries) had known, they would not have crucified the Lord of Glory. In other words, if the devil knew what he was doing, he wouldn't have done it. You talk about a life-altering, incredible mistake. When the devil crucified Jesus, he took on more trouble than he could handle because he crucified a sinless man, and sinless men are not committed to death. Sin is what condemns you to death. Since Jesus never sinned, He went to hell illegally, and that is how He triumphed over hell. The mystery is the Gospel.

The Bible says the mystery of the Gospel is not only what Christ did there, but it is Christ in you, the hope of glory (Colossians 1:27). That is the mystery. Not only did Jesus defeat the devil, but He can now move inside you and give you the power to do it, too. That is the mystery. These are the unsearchable riches: the mystery of Christ in you. That you could be born again—a child of God—and have heaven forever and the devil under your feet. Through the name of Jesus, you have as much power as He had on this earth.

Now, the devil's afraid of that fact, and he fears you knowing it. Satan wants to tell you that you don't have that power, but you do. Absolutely you do. It's time to say to the devil, *"We have been tampered with, Mr. Devil, so don't try to tell us we don't have it because we know we do."*

When the children of God understand who they are and step up and take their place, putting the devil on the run, there is nothing he can do about it. He can't stop it! He is not in control! He is not in authority! He is a defeated foe! He is **not going to** be defeated; he's **already been** defeated. He is already under your feet. Colossians 1:13 says we have been delivered from the authority of darkness and translated into the kingdom of God's dear Son. We are in control now.

Let's look at those verses in Ephesians again:

> And to make all men see what is the fellowship of the mystery, which **from the beginning of the world** hath been hid in God, who created all things by Jesus Christ: **To the intent** that now unto the principalities and powers in heavenly places might be known by the church the manifold wisdom of God (Ephesians 3:9-10, emphasis added).

Before the foundation of the world, the mystery is that Christ **will be in you**. This is past tense now; as a Christian, He **is** in you now.

In this passage, Paul said these words: "to the intent." His intention in telling them this was to take them on a journey to get to this point. Paul said, *"I told you about this—the unsearchable riches of Christ: Christ is in you, the hope of glory—to get to this point."*

We see here that he mentions the "principalities and powers in heavenly places." Those entities can be good or bad—angels or demons—with demons just being fallen angels.

Angels are not omnipotent—they don't know everything. They are not all-knowing. They are servants of the Most High. You, who are in Christ Jesus, have been raised above angels and have more authority than they do. Not more power, but more authority. The angels excel in strength that you don't have. Their power allows them to do things you can't, but Jesus gave us more authority.

The Bible says that these angels take their marching orders—either good or bad—from you. Paul said, *"I told you all these things to the intent—my intention in telling you this was so they know what to do."*

Angels will stand idly by and let you destroy your life unless you put them to work by the words of your mouth. They will not protect or help you **until you let them**. Hebrews 1:14 says, "Are they not all ministering spirits, sent forth to minister for them who shall be heirs of salvation?" They are God's servants, but He has sent them to minister to you. So therefore, they are your servants. Angels were sent to you, awaiting instructions concerning what to do. What are you going to tell them?

One might say, *"Well, I guess we will never make it here in our household. I don't know what we're going to do. Things are bad. My 401K is really going down, and I don't know what I'm going to do. I can't get a job anywhere."* To the extent of what you just said, angels see that as your intention, so that is exactly what they help you accomplish. That truth sheds a different light on things!

Making the Scripture Yours

God's angels will not help you accomplish that negative stuff, but the fallen ones will get after it in a hurry. However, things will change when you stand up and say:

> *Today I'll take my place in Christ. I believe I will be the head, not the tail, above and not beneath. I will be blessed going in and coming out, on the top and not on the bottom. Today I'll take my place in Christ Jesus and be more than a conqueror.*

Someone else might say:

> *Every time we get a little snow, I don't know what happens to me. My body chills, and I get so sick. I don't know what I'm going to do. It happens to me every year. When spring comes, I get a spring cold.*

Is this really what you want to be saying? Well, next time, just refuse to take that cold. Instead, why don't you decide today that you're going to take your place in God—with the intent that those mighty angels are waiting for you?

The Bible says that the angels desire to look into the things that go on in church so they will know what to do with their time. So, they listen to sermons and say, *"Let's go fulfill that today."* They get orders and instructions there. When we say, *"Jesus is Lord over this region. The economy in our city is good. Home sales are up, and my home is selling."* Angels get their instructions at church from your mouth.

> To the intent that now unto the principalities and powers in heavenly places might be known by the church the manifold wisdom of God (Ephesians 3:10).

The wisdom of God is those unsearchable riches—your place in Christ Jesus, the mystery of the Gospel, and all those things wrought in you through Christ Jesus when God raised Him from the dead and gave His power to you—to those of us who believe. Ephesians 1:19 in the King James Version says to "usward," meaning believers.

Here's The Living Bible's translation:

> I pray that you will begin to understand how incredibly great his power is to help those who believe him. It is that same mighty power that raised Christ from the dead and seated him in the place of honor at God's right hand in heaven (Ephesians 1:19-20, TLB).

If you read that prayer in Ephesians 1, you will see how incredible it is. Paul said in Ephesians 1:16, "Cease not to give thanks for you, making mention of you in my prayers." So, if Paul can make mention of me in his prayers, then I can mention you in my prayers as well.

If this is a God-ordained prayer inspired by the Holy Ghost, we should be praying this one. If you want a change in your life that is clear and something you can see, start praying this every day. You have not even imagined what is getting ready to happen to you if you do. Believe me; I have been praying this prayer for over thirty years, and I do not quit. This one will work!

Look at this passage in context:

> Cease not to give thanks for you, making mention of you in my prayers; That the God of our Lord Jesus Christ, the Father of glory, may give unto you the spirit of wisdom and revelation in the knowledge of him: The eyes of your understanding being enlightened; that ye may know what is the hope of his calling, and what the riches of the glory of his inheritance in the saints, And what is the exceeding greatness of his power to us-ward who believe, according to the working of his mighty power, Which he wrought in Christ, when he raised him from the dead, and set him at his own right hand in the heavenly places, Far above all principality, and power, and might, and dominion, and every name that is named, not only in this world, but

also in that which is to come: And hath put all things under his feet, and gave him to be the head over all things to the church, Which is his body, the fulness of him that filleth all in all (Ephesians 1:16-23).

This is how I personalize these verses:

*That the God of **my** Lord Jesus Christ, the Father of glory, may give unto me the spirit of wisdom and revelation may give unto **me** the spirit of wisdom and revelation in the knowledge of Him. That the eyes of **my** understanding may be enlightened. That **I** may know what is the hope of His calling and what the riches of the glory of His inheritance is in the saints. And what is the exceeding greatness of His power toward **me** as a believer, according to the working of His mighty power. Which He wrought in Christ when He raised Him from the dead and set Him at His own right hand in the heavenly places, far above all principality.*

This passage is talking about revelation and the power toward me as a believer; this is what He gave us. Do you know what revelation is? It is knowing. We are not in the dark; we are getting a revelation. I want to know what I have and what to do with it. The power in me is that which He wrought in Christ when He raised Him from the dead. My God! Those principalities must pay attention to me. How about that!

> Far above all principality, and power, and
> might, and dominion, and every name that's
> named, not only in this world, but also in that
> which is to come (Ephesians 1:21).

So, every name that is named in this world is under the name of Jesus, who lives in me. Cancer is a name. Heart trouble is a name. Depression is a name. Anxiety is a name. Fear is a name. All these things are subject to the Greater One who lives in me, and lives in you, too.

And when you know it—really know it—you get hard to handle. So, the only chance the devil has got on you is to get you all religious and get you to believe it's not so. The only chance he has is to tell you that it's not true because he can't stop you if you know it and believe it. His days of beating you are over! Let's continue personalizing these verses:

> *And hath put all things under His feet. The*
> *power which He wrought in Christ when He*
> *raised Him from the dead, set Him at His own*
> *right hand in heavenly places, put Him above*
> *all principality and power and dominion, all*
> *those things, put everything under His feet.*

I'm in His body—the body of Christ—so He's put all things under my feet and gave me to be the head over all things.

The King James Version says, "And hath put all things under his feet, and gave him **to** be the head over all things to the church" (Ephesians 1:22, emphasis added). However, this is not a good translation because the word **"to"** should have been translated as **"for."** So, all the raising up in heavenly places, all this that was put under His feet, all this He wrought in Christ when He raised Him from the dead, God did for the church. He already had all this stuff before the foundation of the world; everything He did was for you.

If He did it for me, I'm taking it. If that's what it cost Him to get it to me, I'm taking it. That's my place. I have every right to have that place.

We talk about these things even though it's hard to say, but it's true because it's in the Bible. We talk about the fullness of the Godhead was bodily in Him: Father, Son, and Holy Ghost; the fullness of the Godhead bodily dwells in Christ Jesus. That's what the Bible says.

Now, look at this next verse: "Which is his body, the fulness of him that filleth all in all" (Ephesians 1:23). For those in the Body of Christ, you have the fullness of the Godhead bodily living in you. It's not just in Him; it's in you, too. The fullness of the Godhead dwells in me. That is not sacrilegious to say because I just read that from the Bible.

Now again, that King James wording is a little hard to decipher. The word "filleth" in Ephesians 1:23 would be better translated *fulfill*. What God is saying is this: *"I have a plan on the earth that cannot be fulfilled until My kids understand who they are and who is living in them."*

Who You Are

God is going to fulfill His plan. He is not going to rain His glory down from heaven; He's going to flow it out of you. He is going to fill us, and His glory will come through the believer who knows who they are in Christ Jesus. That is what speaking the Word does.

The Bible is talking about your place. This is who you are. When we get determined, we are going to the top. There is no economic measure that can put you on top; it's your faith that puts you on top. No legislation can put you on top; faith in God will put you on top. This is who you are, not who you are trying to be. This is absolutely who you already are. You just have to know it.

The devil tries to keep you blind to this fact; he does not want you to believe it. Satan wants to get you to say, *"I'm just a weak beggar trudging through the heat and the cold. We're just going through this world as pilgrims and strangers. At the end of the journey it'll be worth it all."* True, it will be worth it at the end of the journey, but it's also worth it at the beginning. God wants to give you a little heaven on earth.

When you understand who you are in Christ and take your authority, you can't let anything stop you. In fact, nothing can stop you unless you let it. Those angels are standing there right now, waiting for marching orders from you. They will meet you at the door and say, *"What do you want us to do?"*

Do you want a good job, or do you just want to barely make it? Do you want to live in the projects or above them? Do you want a good education, or do you just want to get by? What do you want?

Someone might answer, *"Well, nobody in my family has ever…"* I am not ridiculing anyone's family, but if your family heritage is not what you need it to be, take your family heritage from your heavenly family. You are not limited; the devil just wants to tell you that you are. When you change your thinking, all the other things begin to turn for your good.

SPEAKING FAITH-FILLED WORDS

6

IN THE BEGINNING

God did not create the universe because He is endued with great size. Somehow, humans are constrained by size—things must fit our frame. You have an automobile that is a specific size because it fits you. Your sofa is a certain size because that is what it takes for you to sit or nap comfortably. Our lives are filled with things that are sized to fit us. When we encounter something larger than normal, we must get a tool, ladder, or some other implement to use it. Humans have certain limitations, and we automatically assume that God is restricted by the same things constraining us.

God created this universe not because He is large but because He is wise and powerful. So, when He said, *"I formed you in My image,"* He is not merely talking about your size or appearance; God is talking about things that He put inside you that are like Him. God is a Spirit, and He gave us an expression of Himself through His Son, who we saw in bodily form. Jesus became someone with whom we could identify—someone we could look to and understand.

There is an understanding of God far beyond that accepts His mind and His ways live in you. In the beginning, when God made man, He breathed the breath of life into him. He did not breathe into him so that He could inflate his lungs and start his heart; God breathed into man the essence of Himself and put His Spirit inside him. The breath of God became the life of man.

The way God acts is how we are supposed to act, and the way God did things is also how we are supposed to do them. We are not all-powerful as He is, but we do have power, and we are also all-powerful in Him. **In Him**.

We do have the capacity to do things the way He did—albeit in a limited fashion because of our understanding, restrictions, and confinements. For example, we live in a four-dimensional world—height, width, depth, and time—but there is proof that God lives in at least eleven dimensions. I have heard there is mathematical proof of God living in up to nineteen dimensions, and every time you add a dimension, the possibilities go up astronomically.

If we lived in a two-dimensional world, we would all be flat on the canvas; you cannot emerge. With every dimension, you add new possibilities; add another dimension, and another, and still another dimension, and it is beyond human comprehension. So, we are limited by things that do not limit God. However, in the realm where we live, we still work and act as He does. We function the way God does in the world He gave us.

Creation and Man

In the beginning, God said let there be light, and there was light. Think about this. Genesis 1:1 says, "In the beginning…" This beginning was long ago; in this context, it was before creation as we know it.

One side of a controversy says, "*Well, the earth is very old, and a lot of you creationist and Bible people say the earth is only 6,000 years old, and that can't be true.*" Bible people do not say the earth is only 6,000 years old. No thinking person says that because, in the beginning, God created the heaven and the earth—without definition. Then, creation began to define the earth and the heaven. God's Word says:

> In the beginning God created the heaven and the earth. And the earth was without form, and void; and darkness was upon the face of the deep. And the Spirit of God moved upon the face of the waters. And God said, Let there be light: and there was light (Genesis 1:1-3).

Interestingly, God said, "Let there be light." Later, He said, "*Let there be a greater light by day and a lesser light by night*"— talking about the sun, moon, and stars. So, when God created light in the beginning, He was not talking about the sun, moon, and stars because this command came before they existed.

When scientists try to produce life, they can only go through the motions to somewhat create "life" in a test tube. They can only put the properties together that allow life to emerge, but science has no capacity to truly create life. The Bible says life is in the seed, and once a seed is given the proper environment, life happens.

So, God set things in motion and gave man the power to manipulate them to a degree, but man has no power to create life. Man has no power or ability to go back to that original process where life was created. He can use DNA and run tests on it. He can manipulate it to the point where you get a hybrid peach without fuzz or a watermelon with no seeds. With all that said, they cannot create life. There must be an origin that comes from the Creator God.

In man's search for the origin of life, many intelligent people with years of study on the topic have concluded that **life is light.** When they bring life back to its simplest common denominator, they conclude that life is light. That's right, light. So, when God said "light be," He was breathing life into whatever His voice had influence over.

The universe could be likened to your kitchen table as you sit there using it as a hobby bench. First, you go to the hobby store and buy a model airplane kit in a box. Sitting at the table, you put all the little pieces together. You put the glue in the right places, paint it, and place decals in their correct positions, and you get it to where this boxed-up kit looks great. The end result is a model airplane. It started as a kit in a box, but to a degree, it's your creation. It was not in a usable, presentable form until it had your touch on it. Even though you didn't create the model, you assembled it, so you participated in the creation process.

Now, if someone came up to you and said, *"That's your creation,"* you could say, to a degree, that statement is true. You put it together. Is that your whole universe? No, it is just one little thing.

You must understand that God did not come into being when the universe, as we know it, came into being. From our example, the cosmos was something God assembled on His kitchen table—the whole thing. His creation had light years expanding out by the second.

Experts say the Big Bang Theory is feasible because they can study the movement of the solar system and trace it back to the point of origin; it started in a particular place. One of the reasons they can discover the source is due to the continuous movement; it continues to exude out from its starting place.

The universe is still expanding at the speed of light in all directions and has for eons. Comparatively speaking, when you sit at the table and begin to put the model airplane together—it's the beginning, and that is what the Bible refers to in Genesis. It is not the beginning of God; it is just the beginning of this thing that He lets you use. But, for understanding, it is really a science project. I am talking about the whole deal; I am not talking about you. You are a part of it, but this whole thing was put here by Someone who is intelligent. The Bible says that this universe and this world were created by the wisdom of God; it was not created because God's big.

The point here is that God showed us some principles that He used **in the beginning** of it all. He used them in the beginning —in the beginning of life—and we can use these same principles in the beginning of your project, the beginning of your challenge, the beginning of your difficulty, the beginning of your crisis, the beginning of your unwelcome news—and not at the end.

SPEAKING FAITH-FILLED WORDS

7

THE SUBSTANCE OF FAITH

Hebrews chapter 11 is what we refer to as the "faith chapter" of the Bible. In this book, God gives us an illustration of speaking faith-filled words. It says:

> "**Now** faith is the substance of things hoped
> for, the evidence of things not seen"
> (Hebrews 11:1, emphasis added).

Scripture says that faith is a substance. For example, when you went to the hobby store, brought home the model plane kit, laid it out on the table, and started your project, that was substance. Therefore, you must begin with substance.

The Bible says that where we live—our planet, the universe— was created from something called substance. For our understanding, God called this substance "faith." Some people might want to argue with you about this, but remember, we read it straight from the Bible. If we read it from Golf Magazine™, you could just forget it. But we didn't read it there; we read it directly from God's Word.

This verse also says, "Now faith is," or you could say it this way, *"Faith is now."* Now faith is; faith is now. That is not a violation. So, if it's not now, it's not faith. In other words, to say *"God will do it someday"* is not faith.

If it is not NOW, it is not faith.

Some may say, *"I believe I'm going to get my healing someday."* Sorry pal, you're not going to get it—not according to that statement. You might get it some other way, such as by God giving you a miracle or by Him granting you some grace, but you are not going to get it through faith. When you believe that you **are going to get** something someday, you are not believing in faith because if it is not now, it is not faith. It must be now before faith works. You must believe you receive when you pray, not when you see it manifested. You must believe it before you see it. The Bible says that faith is the substance of things hoped for now.

Begin to Believe

God has put inside you the capacity to imagine. In 2 Corinthians 10:5, we are told to cast down imaginations that exalt themselves against the knowledge of God. You have been given an imagination. Inside that imagination, God has given you the ability to dream. Not only has He given you the ability to dream, but He has also given you the ability to hear His voice.

So, God will come to you in a dream—not necessarily a dream in the night, but it could be. He will come to you with something you begin to believe before you see it. You start to believe in your future before you have it or believe something is possible before it manifests. You believe you can have an excellent job when you don't have one. You believe you can have a bright future when it looks like your life is the antithesis. You begin to believe you can graduate from college before you ever enroll. You begin believing—having a dream or vision—and start to see your future before it happens; that is hope. **Hope** is a favorable expectation. A lack of hope is an unfavorable expectation.

When someone comes to you and gives you unwelcome news and steals your hope, you begin to believe the future is going to work negatively. For example, a doctor comes to you with a negative diagnosis concerning a loved one and says there is no hope for them to live. When the doctor declares "no hope," the atmosphere changes.

On the flip side of the coin, the doctor comes up to you and says, *"Everything went great; things are going to be fine. There are no problems and no lasting impact. We'll be through here in about two hours, and you can take them home."* That report is a relief to hear. It brings a new set of emotions; you have a different hope and a different vision. Inside, you see something different from what you initially thought.

In other words, faith gives substance to how you want it to be. A person may say, *"Well, I'm believing for the bad."* Along with that being incredibly unwise, your belief will be successful. **The question is not whether you are going to use your faith; it's whether or not you are going to use your faith correctly.** It is not whether you are using it; you are using it. If you put hope in the news media for your assessment of the future, you have a real problem. However, I'm going to put my hope in God's Word; I am going to put my hope in the Lord.

So, faith is the substance of things hoped for, the evidence of things not seen. The substance we are working with is invisible to us, but that does not mean it does not exist. God has put something invisible under our control. This invisible substance is the same thing He used to create the universe!

God used faith, formulated it, and controlled its parameters and boundaries. He said, *"You can come this far and no farther."* He created a boundary. He saw the vision of it before He said it. The ocean can't go anywhere it wants; He put a barrier up and said, *"I separated the land from the sea."* He used His words like an artist uses a brush. He created and painted what He wanted.

Hebrews 11:3 says, "Through faith we understand that the worlds were framed by the word of God..." This verse illustrates what I said in the preceding paragraph. The King James translation misses it a little because it makes you think: Through faith we understand, period. We use our faith so we can understand. However, this is **not** what that verse says. It says that through faith the worlds were framed. It isn't our faith that allows us to understand. No, it's that we understand that God, using His faith, framed the worlds.

We must understand that there is a difference between **the faith of God** and **having faith in God**. We, being the lesser, must put faith in God, the greater. I acknowledge that I can't save myself, so I put faith in God, the Greater One, who can save me. God does not need saving, so He does not have to put faith in anyone; He has faith.

When we come into God's family, we get His faith. The Bible says, "For by grace are ye saved through faith; and that not of yourselves: it is the **gift of God**" (Ephesians 2:8, emphasis added). His faith is put in us at salvation, and He gives us the tools to use that faith.

The faith in you—that saved you—is a gift from God. God has given you faith; in fact, He put His faith in you and told you to use your faith like He uses His. Here's an example: We understand that through faith the worlds were painted as an artist would use a paintbrush—the King James translation says "framed." You put a frame around a picture. The artist used the brush to form what he wanted, and he used an invisible substance—invisible to us. The clay He took off the shelf became the things that we see. Everything came from it. So, the clay on the shelf is this thing called faith. It is the substance of your hope that brings it to pass.

Faith in God

How would you want your future to look? Are you happy with it as it is, or would you like to make a change? Are you pessimistic about the future? I am concerned about the world, but God said to "be of good cheer."

> These things I have spoken unto you, that in me ye might have peace. In the world ye shall have tribulation: **but be of good cheer; I have overcome the world** (John 16:33, emphasis added).

Our future is bright. We are not bound to this world, and faith is not bound to the economics of this world. God is smart. He took the children of Israel—who borrowed the Egyptian's substance—into the desert where there was nothing to buy. You can have all the money in the world and no place to spend it: no malls, no restaurants, no takeout, no movies, nothing. God gives the Israelites all the money, and there is nothing to spend it on. They took the entire economy of Egypt, the wealth of the greatest nation on the planet, into a place God directed where there was absolutely nothing to spend it on. They were out there for forty years with all that wealth. Talk about money burning a hole in your tunic! There is nothing to spend it on, but they probably traded a bit.

Then God tells them, *"I'm going to feed you with manna from heaven."* They have all the money in the world and no place to spend it, and God is going to feed them, too! This story is a perfect illustration of not being dependent on the world's economy. Manna is still available to us if needed.

God's promise to meet your need according to His riches in glory by Christ Jesus (Philippians 4:19) is not dependent on the U. S. Government, the stock market, the Federal Reserve, the banking system, or any other financial vehicle. He gave you a covenant that is higher and greater than it all so that you wouldn't be dependent on any of it. God wants you to know that you don't have to rely on these things.

Naturally speaking, I lost a lot of money in the current economic times. However, the same God who gave me that money is the same God who will provide me with more if needed.

Our faith is put in so many things other than God. We begin to depend on things that cannot sustain us, but God says His covenant with you will sustain and uphold you.

The invisible clay sitting on the shelf is the substance whereby all of this was created. God gives you access to the invisible clay through the process called faith. This is how the Word of God framed the worlds.

SPEAKING FAITH-FILLED WORDS

8

TALK ABOUT YOUR VICTORY

> In the beginning God created the heaven and the earth. And the earth was without form, and void; and darkness was upon the face of the deep. And the Spirit of God moved upon the face of the waters. And God said... (Genesis 1:1-3a).

Notice in this passage of Scripture that nothing happened until God spoke. What is going to happen for you? Same thing. Nothing, not until you say something.

If you don't start talking your victory, nothing is going to happen for you, either. You will go along struggling, and life will be a burden to you—a millstone around your neck. You will hate getting up day after day after day until you change what you say. However, when you begin to change what you say, you have entered the process of coming out.

We are the sum total of our words, but let's be clear, words are not the only thing that controls our future; actions also have much to do with it. Your mind and actions must be in line with the Word of God. Speaking God's Word and never acting like it's true won't work for you. You must have action involved with your faith.

You can't keep saying, *"I'm a college grad; I'm a college grad; I'm a college grad,"* and never apply to a school. Your actions need to be consistent with your words. You must begin to act on what you say, and what you say should be in line with what God says.

An Artist's Creation

> And God said, Let there be light: and there was light. And God saw the light, that it was good: and God divided the light from the darkness. And God called the light Day, and the darkness he called Night. And the evening and the morning were the first day. And God said, Let there be a firmament in the midst of the waters, and let it divide the waters from the waters... And God said, Let the waters under the heaven be gathered together unto one place, and let the dry land appear: and it was so (Genesis 1:3-6, 9).

God gathered the waters, and the land emerged. That action was the artist creating—using the clay to form the image He wants. The worlds were framed, formed, and created. The artist took the brush and painted it.

Then the Bible says the earth brings forth grass. In verse 14, the sun and moon were created. Light already existed, so the sun and the moon were not the lights God created in verse 3; there was light before the sun and moon. Next, He told the waters to bring forth abundantly and then commanded all living creatures to produce after their own kind. Finally, we see the creation of man, "And God said, Let us make man in our image…" (Genesis 1:26).

God created everything piece by piece. It is like that model airplane we talked about earlier. You took the pieces out of the box and laid all the contents on the table. You looked carefully at the parts representing the fuselage, which houses the cockpit, the cargo bay, and the area designated for the passengers. Then you looked at the wings, empennage, engines, propellers, and landing gear. You start the process of putting the pieces together, taking the interior parts and putting them in place—seats, cockpit, landing gear, and wheels. You must put all that in before you can assemble the plane correctly. The artist creates the intricate details.

Various artistic methods combined with the creative ability of the one with the brush has a power in it. There is something the artist is trying to put on the canvas. They will step back from it, and after perusing it, they take their brush and make one little stroke here and another one there.

Then with absolutely no idea about what the artist wants, someone comes along and draws a mustache on it! In the same way, the people trying to ruin it are those saying things to you against what you are trying to create—the mustache on the painting. People ruin it when someone tells you how to use your faith in a wrong way—against what God intended. It may not have been what you wanted, but you were influenced.

When God told Abraham that He was going to bless him, He made him leave the land where he was and his family because they were getting ready to draw a mustache on his painting. God said, "Wherefore come out from among them..." (2 Corinthians 6:17). Abraham's family wanted to make something that was never intended.

Sometimes you have to step back because you are being influenced in a way that is going to take you somewhere you don't want to go. It begins with them getting you to use **your own words** against you. However, their words will not stop you, but they may slow you down a bit. The faith of another cannot overcome your faith. Negative faith cannot overcome yours. Cream, given enough time, will always rise to the top. Your environment can hold you down for a little while, but it cannot completely stop you.

> ## Another person's faith cannot overcome yours.

So, God began by speaking one thing, then another, and little by little, His creation—His artwork—became more defined and detailed, becoming more precisely what He wanted.

He went through the process of creation, and God said let us make man in our image. Time and again, He looked back over His creation and declared it all good with one exception. As He looked back at the creation of man, He said, *"That's not so good."* In other words, God was saying, *"I have created all this with My canvas laid out. I have the fish, birds, fowl, and cattle in place; I even have the creeping things. I created this pristine, pure environment for man."* His creation was good enough before man got there, but after man arrived, it was no longer good enough.

This is the reason why God must take you to a new place called heaven because no matter what you get on this earth, it's not good enough for you. Someone may say, *"You can't say that!"* But you most certainly can say it because we are created in the image and likeness of God; there's greatness on the inside of you. No matter what this world has, it is not good enough for you. You are created to live beyond the stars; you are created for greatness. You are created in the image and likeness of the Most High God.

The Devil Says You're Not Worthy

Then the question arises: Does God wants us to prosper? My answer to that is: He has only created a new universe for you! Do you think He might want you to prosper? Do you believe it is even a question? I just don't understand the person who asks that. I do not understand why that question even comes up. Somebody has not been reading their Bible.

"Do you think God would give me a new house?" Seriously? The devil's answer is: *"No, God wouldn't do that. You might have gone a little overboard now."*

"Do you think God would give me a new car?" Satan answers: *"Absolutely not! God wants the devil's crowd to drive all of them. He wants only the entertainers, movie stars, and drug dealers to drive them."*

"Do you think God would let me have a closet full of nice new clothes? Maybe even some Bespoke™ suits?" The devil asks: *"Are*

you out of your mind? God wouldn't even think of doing that for you. Your whole family lived poor all their lives. Why would He want to do that for you?"

The devil says, *"You are nothing special."* He doesn't want you to find out who you really are. The thing he has been trying to keep from you your whole life is how worthy you are. He tells you the opposite—that you are unworthy. Satan tells you that you can't do it and will always be at the bottom.

Let me tell you about warfare. Warfare is designed to keep you believing you are a nobody. Government handouts are to get you dependent on your sugar daddy instead of your God. I do not need their bailout; I don't want their crumbs. The Lord has prepared a table for us in the presence of our enemies, and I am coming to the table. If you don't want to come and eat, don't go, but I'm eating. I'm going to the table in a hurry. Pass the steak and potatoes!

Pleasing God

When you speak faith-filled words, it pleases God; it does not anger Him. Faith-filled words have power when you talk about your victories and your ability to overcome. We need to speak the way that God wants us to speak. Tell the devil that he has no right to take over; he has come far enough. The Bible says that my tongue is as the pen of a ready writer inditing a good matter (Psalm 45:1). I have a future and a hope.

Begin to create your world. You start to paint your world with the words of your mouth like God created and painted this world where we live. You have the clay on the shelf—your faith. Reach up there, pull it down, and begin to create the world you want. Are you going to let the news media create your world, or will you create your own? It's up to us. God said He has put faith on the inside of you. Now, what are you going to do with it?

9

MY CONFESSION OF FAITH

The Bible says we believe, and therefore we speak. What you believe is what you begin to say. You have to put the devil's lies in their place. Begin to tell him: *I'm getting promoted. Others are getting laid off, but I believe I'm going to get promoted today… No, I don't think I'll get the Covid virus. Not today. That is not my image of hope for my future… No, I don't think I'll receive cancer today.*

Not any day.

Someone might tell you, *"You may die from cancer."* But my *response is: "I may live, too!"* You can't kill people who won't die. Study some of the martyrs or certain people in the New Testament. For example, the Romans could not kill the apostle John, so the Emperor exiled him to the Isle of Patmos, where he authored the Book of Revelation for us; he couldn't be stopped even when they exiled him. They tried to kill him before they exiled him by boiling him in oil, and **he would not die**. He would not die! You do not have to die until you want to die, even if others say you will die. The power of life and death is in the tongue. Tell them, *"I am not going to die on your timetable."* You are not done yet!

| You can't kill people who won't die. |

I am not trying to be arrogant or flippant, but I refuse to die just *because somebody says I will.* You ask, *"Well,* **what about** *all these people who died?"* I can't build my faith on the *"what abouts."* The Bible says faith comes by hearing and hearing by the Word of God. It did not say that faith comes by hearing the *"what abouts."*

Others want to counter and say, *"Well, So-and-So was a good Christian, and they died."* Here's a news flash: All good Christians will die sometime. I heard about a person who said to the famous evangelist Oral Roberts, *"You laid hands on all those people, and I know one of them who died."* Oral Roberts replied, *"Listen pal, everyone I lay hands on dies eventually."* Death is coming to all of us, but the Bible says God satisfies us with long life. If you are not satisfied, you do not have to die. If you are not done, don't quit. Don't give up. Don't throw in the towel. It's not over for you until you say it's over.

Speak to It

Just as God breathed into you the breath of life, He breathed into you the power to act just like He does. Speak to the mountain: Be removed and cast into the sea, and it will obey you. Just like Jesus spoke to the fig tree, and it withered up from the root. When His disciples asked Him about it, He answered, "…ye shall not only do this which is done to the fig tree, but also if ye shall say unto this mountain, Be thou removed, and be thou cast into the sea; it shall be done" (Matthew 21:21).

Do you remember what Jesus said to His disciples when they brought Him a child that needed healing? They couldn't heal the boy because he had a devil, and they couldn't cast it out. So, Jesus said, "O faithless and perverse generation, how long shall I be with you?" (Matthew 17:17). In other words, Jesus rebuked them saying, *"How long is it going to take until you get this? How long do I have to be with you? You possess all the power to do something about this, but you will not do it. You don't know what to do with what's inside you. I put it in you; it's there. Now, what are you going to do with it?"*

Another time, the boat was on the water, tossed with the winds, going up and down, and they were all afraid. But where was Jesus? He was in the back of the boat asleep. Then, finally, they woke Him and declared, *"Don't you care? We're going to drown."* He responded with something like, *"What's with you guys? What is going on here? Don't you know you can have what you say?"* My paraphrase.

Jesus spoke to the wind and the sea, and they calmed down at once, and the boat was found on the other side. I don't know how that happened, but it did. Jesus was in the boat, sleeping and expecting them to be the ones to speak to the wind and waves. But, He had to get up and do it Himself.

Today, He wants us to speak to the wind and the waves. Speak to the economy. Talk to your future. Start speaking to your family. Start speaking to your job. Start speaking to your body. Do you need Him to come and do it for you, or are you going to use what He gave you? That's what He's saying in these examples.

The book of Hebrews says that it is time for you to be teaching others, but you still need others to teach you again:

For when for the time ye ought to be teachers,
ye have need that one teach you again which be
the first principles of the oracles of God..."
(Hebrews 5:12).

Do you have to go back and go over this repeatedly, or will you put into practice what you already know?

My Confession of Faith

I don't know what the future is going to look like because God has hidden it from us to a degree so that we move in faith. But I promise you, as surely as the sun comes up tomorrow, I will overcome. I will be the head and not the tail. I will be above and not beneath. I will be blessed going in and coming out. The labor of my hand is blessed. I don't know what things are going to look like, and I don't know every detail, but I am going to be more than a conqueror through Christ Jesus. I will win, and I will not lose. I will overcome and go to the other side. I will have plenty to eat. I will have a place to stay. I will have a good fruitful career. I will have what I need to live this life. He has given me all things that pertain to life and godliness; I have everything I need and then some.

He told me in His Word that it is His will that I prosper and be in health. So, I **will** prosper and be in health. I don't know about all the other details, but that is what I will have. I will have what I say, and that is what I say. I will overcome; I will be a victor. I will be more than a conqueror.

I am a world overcomer. Are you? You can have what you say.

Someone might say that you can't know about all this, but my answer is: I do know because nothing I said is based on anything I have done. I said it based on my covenant with Almighty God, and He is more than able. He watches over His Word to perform it. He is waiting. The angels are coming to attention and saying, *"Yeah! Go! Run and get it."* All things are working together for my good because I'm called according to His purpose.

I shared my confession of faith with you; now, take the time to make it yours. We are going to win! We are not going to lose!

10

FAITH IS ALIVE

> Now faith is the substance of things hoped for,
> the evidence of things not seen. For by it [faith]
> the elders obtained a good report. Through faith
> we understand that the worlds were framed by
> the word of God, so that things which are seen
> were not made of things which do appear... But
> without faith it is impossible to please him [God]:
> for he that cometh to God must believe that he is,
> and that he is a **rewarder** of them that diligently
> seek him (Hebrews 11:1-3, 6, emphasis added).

Underscore those verses in your thinking. The reward God is talking about here is not your heavenly reward; it is talking about the reward of faith as it works here on this earth. The entire chapter 11 of Hebrews deals with the subject of faith.

The Bible says that whatsoever is not of faith—proceeds not from faith—is sin. Some people will tell you that the faith message is dead. But how can anything be dead that pleases God and that He requires us to utilize? However, there are times and seasons in the body of Christ when the Lord emphasizes certain things above others. There may be a season where He focuses on a particular thing. Often, God's reason for doing that is because there has been a void or something is missing in the body of Christ, and He must hammer it home until the principle is reiterated and the point gets made.

When the season passes, and He backs off one topic and emphasizes another, that does not mean the previous truth is irrelevant. It just means that we should have learned it by then. Sometimes we let these truths get a little cloudy by reading them like catchphrases or clichés, and God wants us to stop and take thought of their meanings. So, faith is not dead. It could not be dead as long as the Bible is alive because faith comes by hearing and hearing by the Word of God.

Out of the Abundance of the Heart

The Bible teaches that the Word of God is like a seed, and the sower sows that seed or God's Word. Then we learn that satan comes immediately to take away the Word that was planted. Let's look at it in the book of Mark:

> The sower soweth the word. **And these are they by the way side, where the word is sown; but when they have heard, Satan cometh immediately, and taketh away the word that was sown in their hearts.** And these are they likewise which are sown on stony ground; who, when they have heard the word, immediately receive it with gladness; And have no root in themselves, and so endure but for a time: afterward, when **affliction or persecution**

ariseth for the word's sake, immediately they are offended (Mark 4:14-17, emphasis added).

How does satan try to steal the Word? Jesus talks about how he does it through persecution, affliction, cares of this world, deceitfulness of riches, and lusts of other things. Those are the five things the devil uses to steal the Word.

This passage in Mark goes into detail:

> And these are they which are sown among thorns; such as hear the word, And the cares of this world, and the deceitfulness of riches, and the lusts of other things entering in, choke the word, and it becometh unfruitful. And these are they which are sown on good ground; such as hear the word, and receive it, and bring forth fruit, some thirtyfold, some sixty, and some an hundred (Mark 4:18-20).

When you go to the next passage, the subject does not change. The subject is the same, but it sounds like it has changed. Let's look at it:

> And he said unto them, Is a candle brought to be put under a bushel, or under a bed? and not to be set on a candlestick? **For there is nothing hid, which shall not be manifested**; neither was any thing kept secret, but that it should come abroad. If any man have ears to hear, let him hear. And he said unto them, Take heed what ye hear: with what measure ye mete, it shall be measured to you: and unto you that hear shall

more be given. For he that hath, to him shall be given: and he that hath not, from him shall be taken even that which he hath (Mark 4:21-25, emphasis added).

The Bible tells us, "The spirit of man is the **candle** of the Lord, searching all the inward parts of the **belly** (Proverbs 20:27, emphasis added). In today's vernacular, the word "candle" would be a lamp, light, or light bulb.

Rivers of living water flow from your belly (John 7:38). **Belly** refers to your inner man, the core of your being, the essence of who you are.

We are a three-part being. We are a spirit. We have a soul, and we live in a body. You have a soul, and your body is a tool. Your body is not the real you; the real you is your spirit. When your body dies, it is your spirit that continues to live.

So, if the spirit of man is the candle of the Lord, you have some words here that begin to work together. The candle is not to be hidden under a bed or a bushel; it is to be set on a candlestick. In other words, God is saying that the revelation coming to your spirit is not to be hidden. The things you understand on the inside are to dominate and control your life and not take a back seat to the external. The external is not more important than the internal. The internal part of you is the connection point to God. There is nothing to be hidden away on the inside of you.

Continuing in Mark 4, it says, "For there is nothing hid, which shall not be manifested..." (Mark 4:22). Hidden where? Hidden away inside you. You cannot stop what is inside you from coming out. What is in you will come out because from "out of the abundance of the heart the mouth speaketh" (Matthew 12:34). So, what is in you will come out.

Religious Traditions

Let's look at this passage again:

> For there is nothing hid, which shall not be manifested; neither was any thing kept secret, but that it should come abroad. If any man have ears to hear, let him hear (Mark 4:22-23).

In this passage, God is not talking about the ears on the outside of your head; He is talking about the ears of your spirit. Some people hear, and some people do not. I have preached all over the world, and in some places, preaching is like throwing a rubber ball against a brick wall. It comes back faster than it went out. It won't soak in, and it is not received.

The Word of God must be received before it has any power to change us. You will find the most prevalent obstacle that stops us from being able to receive the Word is preconditioning. If you have a prejudice—a prejudgment—against a particular thing, then you won't be able to receive it. Your spirit will be cut off from the ability to attain, retain, or grasp it. You will reject it before it even comes to you.

The most significant contributing factor to our prejudice is usually religion. I say this because we hold religion at a higher level than other routine things of life. If we hear something in a religious context, it automatically gets a higher place, but if it is not biblical, then it's a tradition of men—not the Word of God. Jesus Himself said the traditions of men make the Word of God of no effect (ineffectual) (Mark 7:13). The traditions that people hold to, especially the religious ones, can stop God from doing anything in a person's life. It can cut us off and be difficult to beat it back down. The problem is that sometimes we don't know how much we've been affected because it involves an element of truth. Many times, those traditions turn into a set of religious cliches.

We have these little sayings that we use: *"You never know what God's gonna do"* and other similar aphorisms. Well, that statement is not even remotely true. We know precisely what God is going to do because; He will do exactly what He said in His Word. The only reason you don't know what God's going to do is because you don't know what He said about your situation. But, if you are informed about what He said, you know what He will do. He has already told you.

God said He was not a man that He should lie, and there is neither shadow nor variableness of turning in Him. Therefore, He will do what He said He would do, and we can put confidence in that.

11
DEVELOPING YOUR FAITH

> If any man have ears to hear, let him hear. And
> he said unto them, Take heed what ye hear:
> with what measure ye **mete**, it shall be measured
> to you: and unto you that hear shall more be
> given (Mark 4:23-24, emphasis added).

This passage is talking about what you hear with your spirit.
Mete means: to dispense or allot justice, punishment, or harsh
treatment (OxfordDictionaries@Oxford University Press). An
example would be: "There was punishment **meted** out to the
football kick-off team for allowing a 99-yard run touchdown."

Another example can be found in baking, which can be
challenging. If you bake something and get wrong measurements
or ingredients, you will get wrong results. It will all be wrong.
For example, if you **mete** out salt instead of sugar in a dessert,
you will get something inedible. It is not going to be what you
expect, even though the two ingredients look the same.

These verses are talking about what you hear on the inside.
Jesus said, from a spiritual standpoint, for those who hear right
and respond correctly to what they hear, more shall be given to
them.

God is not saying there are the haves and have-nots; He's not choosing one over another. No, He said the measure **you** mete, it will be measured to you again. If you are a diligent hearer, it will come back to you better than for a casual hearer. The more thought, meditation, and study you give to what you hear will determine how it returns to you.

The God-kind of Faith

> "For he that hath, to him shall be given: and he that hath not, from him shall be taken even that which he hath" (Mark 4:25).

Jesus is not talking about God wanting to take things from you but rather protecting what's going on with the spiritual part of your life. He said you can lose the growth you gained. You don't keep spiritual growth automatically; you must stay on top of it. That is why you don't need to let religion rob you of the Word of God.

Let's look again at chapter eleven of Mark, where Jesus was staying in Bethany at the house of Mary, Martha, and Lazarus (who was raised from the dead). He regularly made the short walk back and forth from Bethany to the temple in Jerusalem.

> And Jesus entered into Jerusalem, and into the temple: and when he had looked round about upon all things, and now the eventide was come, he went out unto Bethany with the twelve. And on the morrow, when they were come from Bethany, he was hungry: And seeing a fig tree afar off having leaves, he came, if haply

[perhaps] he might find any thing thereon: and when he came to it, he found nothing but leaves; for the time of figs was not yet. **And Jesus answered** and said unto it, No man eat fruit of thee hereafter for ever. And his disciples heard it. And they come to Jerusalem: and Jesus went into the temple, and began to cast out them that sold and bought in the temple, and overthrew the tables of the moneychangers, and the seats of them that sold doves (Mark 11:11-15, emphasis added).

Interestingly, Jesus answered a tree. Something was going on in His Spirit regarding that tree. The tree was communicating with Him in some way. There are circumstances in life that will talk to you if you listen. When the Bible says that Jesus answered and spoke to a living but inanimate object, He said it out loud.

If you remember, the Bible says that when the fig tree buds, you know that summer is approaching (Matthew 24). Joel talks about the fig tree, and it's spoken about in other places as well. There is a typology going on here: Jesus is talking to a literal fig tree, but the fig tree also represents the nation of Israel. In reality, He is speaking to a representation of the religious system that had become less than stellar. When He went in and turned over the moneychangers' tables, that fig tree represented what went on in the temple.

And when even was come, he went out of the city. And in the morning, as they passed by, they saw the fig tree dried up from the roots. And Peter calling to remembrance saith unto

> him, Master, behold, the fig tree which thou
> cursedst is withered away. And Jesus answering
> saith unto them, **Have faith in God** (Mark
> 11:19-22, emphasis added).

Jesus spent the day teaching in the temple and returned to Bethany at night. The next day, after Jesus cursed the fig tree, they passed it again.

The disciples observed that the cursed fig tree had withered. Jesus responded to them, "Have faith in God," translated in some versions as, "Have the faith of God." We are to operate in God's faith.

The Measure of Faith

> For by grace are ye saved through faith; and that
> not of yourselves: it is the gift of God: Not of
> works, lest any man should boast (Ephesians
> 2:8-9).

The faith that saved you was a gift from God. The Bible says that all men **among you** have faith. People in the world do not have faith, but God puts faith in you when you are saved.

Scripture also says, "God hath dealt to every man the measure of faith" (Romans 12:3). He did not say **a measure** of faith; He said **the measure** of faith. So, the Bible tells us that every man has been dealt the measure of faith.

There is not a little portion for you and a big portion for another; faith is not variable. God does not dole out a great measure of faith to one person and a tiny little morsel of faith to another. There is this abiding faith that comes to live inside us, and the attention we give to it (like we read in Mark 4) determines how our faith grows. Your relationship with God and the Word and how you protect them determines how faith grows in you. It is not that God created one person with more faith than another. No, every man has been dealt the measure of faith.

> Through faith we understand that the worlds were framed by the word of God, so that things which are seen were not made of things which do appear (Hebrews 11:3).

In other words, what you see here is something not made in its most original form and was not made from something visible. So, when the Bible says that faith is the substance of things hoped for, realize that hope is the vision you have of something before it ever manifests.

For example, before my preaching pulpit was constructed, I created a sketch of it and told the manufacturer what I wanted. Then, the experts put their heads together and showed me a detailed drawing after everything I wanted was added. My sketch was rough, but someone took it and **developed** it. Do you see the word "develop"? We know that Jesus is the author and finisher of your faith. One Bible version translates the word **finisher** as "developer." Faith works in the same way as the example with the pulpit. Initially, faith will be in rough form, but the more you work with it, the more refined or developed it gets; it becomes more exact and precise in what it is capable of doing. As a result, your faith will grow greater and greater. So, your faith can be substantially developed, and you can do more with it.

It takes more work to make a piece of fine furniture than it does to build a sawhorse for working in the garage. It takes more skill. Why? Because it is a more refined product and the processes involved are more intricate, fine furniture takes more skill. In the same way, it takes more work to learn how to use your faith to become usable and more precise in its functioning.

12

USING YOUR FAITH

"Now faith is the substance of things hoped for, the
evidence of things not seen" (Hebrews 11:1).

Hope is the image that you see before anything exists. It's the
way you want something to be. It is the anticipation and the
expectation you have of how it will work out.

When you hope for something, it's not yet seen. When
something is in hope form, it is not seen. Hope is the blueprint
that drives your faith, but hope alone will never get you
anything. I've heard people say, *"We're just wishing and hoping"*
or *"We're just hoping and praying."* Well, they are certainly not
in "getting" mode! They are not going to get anything. God
has not promised to fulfill your hope, but He has promised to
fulfill your faith. Faith is what gives substance to your hope.
Faith is the substance of the things for which you hope.

We read earlier that the Word of God framed the worlds. God
had a hope-image on the inside of Him. In other words, this
is what He hoped the universe would look like before He
started. Then when He had that picture sufficiently painted on
the inside of Him the way He wanted it to be expressed, He
began to speak to it.

In the beginning, God said, *"Let there be light,"* and there was light. In the beginning, He said, *"Let us make man in our image, after our likeness,"* and it happened. God knew what He was saying and used His words, not just in a rough sawhorse version but in a finished fashion that gave us the creation we enjoy today. So, when He breathed in man the breath of life, He breathed in us the ability to use faith the way God uses His.

Faith is this raw product—an invisible raw material that sits on the shelf in your unseen art studio. You cannot see it, but it is the evidence of things not seen. You can't see this substance called faith, but everything that exists came from it. There is a substance—a building block—a building product—called faith that created everything you see. You are sitting in a product that initially came from God's faith on the inside of Him.

God has put that substance on hold for our use. His instructions were something like, *"When you need to create something in your life, pull out the building blocks, pull out the substance called faith, and apply it."* The paintbrush that you use to apply it is your words because your tongue is as the pen of a ready writer inditing a good matter (Psalm 45:1).

Let's look at that verse from a couple of other translations:

> "A marvelous word has stirred my heart as I mention my works to the king. My tongue is the pen of a skillful scribe" (Psalm 45:1, CEB).

> "My heart is overflowing with good news. I will direct my song to the king. My tongue is a pen for a skillful writer" (Psalm 45:1, GW).

My tongue is the pen of a ready writer inditing a good matter. What you say is the material; your faith brings the material onto the scene. That material is unseen, but your faith will eventually make it seen. So, you take it off the shelf and use it.

That substance will sit on the shelf until you put it to work. That substance is there; it exists. It is there to be used by you, but it will never go to work or be applied until you begin to say what you want to happen—your hope.

Negative Faith

> **Faith can just as easily be negative as it can be positive.**

Someone says, *"I'm hoping I'll go broke."* Why do they say it? Why are they putting substance to work against them? Faith can just as easily be negative as it can be positive. Everybody uses faith, but some people put faith in the negative. When you believe that all the undesirable things that can happen to you will happen, that's faith in the negative. So, everyone uses faith; it's just whether they're using it for their benefit or against them, but everybody uses it.

Then they say, *"But I didn't know I was using faith."* Unfortunately, ignorance is no excuse; there are many things we don't know that can kill us. The Scripture says, "My people are destroyed for a lack of knowledge…" (Hosea 4:6a). What you don't know can indeed kill you!

There are many experiences in life that I would have done differently because at the time, I did not know any better. Had

I known, there could have been a different outcome. But because I did not know any better, my ignorance cost me something significant. We are all that way, and you can't go back and undo it. All you can do is chalk it up to experience and resolve never to let it happen again. The price you pay for ignorance—call it tuition—pay it and go on. That's all you can do; you can't change it. It is what it is. It happened, and you must press on.

Learn from your mistakes. Use the faith that God gave us—the substance of things you hope for and the evidence of things not seen. It brings the things you cannot see into evidence, into a place where you can see and hold them.

The Object of Your Faith

If I need to be saved or need God to do something for me that I can't do, that's where I must put faith in Him. We don't pray to the object—a mountain, tree, etc. Likewise, Jesus didn't pray to the fig tree; He answered the tree. He talked to the tree. He didn't pray to it.

> **Don't pray to things; pray to God.**

God is the object of your faith. Have faith in God. I cannot save myself. Jesus is my savior; He is the Lord of my life. When I needed to be saved, I had to call on Him to do what I couldn't do. So, in that regard, I have faith in God.

There is another important thing you must remember about faith. We not only have faith in God, but **we also have the faith of God.** When you were given that gift of faith, it keeps growing. Scripture says that your faith grows exceedingly, and we are to be strong in faith, not weak in faith. The Bible admonishes us to use and increase the faith He gave us. Using Jesus' example, I'm supposed to talk to trees, not pray to them. I pray to God; I speak to trees. So, when I pray to God, I have faith **in God**; when I talk to trees, I use the faith **of God**. They are totally different things.

Speak to Mountains

Now, if you say, *"God, will you move the tree?"* He's going to say, *"No, I'm not going to move the tree."* You must apply your faith to the tree for it to move. Peter reminds Jesus of the fig tree:

> And Peter calling to remembrance saith unto him, Master, behold, the fig tree which thou cursedst is withered away. And Jesus answering saith unto them, **Have faith in God**. For verily **I say unto you,** That **whosoever shall say** unto this mountain, Be thou removed, and be thou cast into the sea; and shall not doubt in his heart, but shall believe that those things which he saith shall come to pass; he shall have whatsoever he saith (Mark 11:21-23, emphasis added).

Instead of being translated as "have faith in God," I think in this application, a better translation would be **"have the faith of God,"** as we said earlier. Some translations translate it like that. So, have the faith of God, referring to the application of an individual's faith toward an object.

This passage does not say, *"For verily I say unto you, that whosoever shall say...**the Heavenly Father**, please move the mountain."* In other words, *"Lord, please move this mountain. Lord, please make this mountain move!"* No, if that verse was written that way, that would be **faith in God** rather than the **faith of God.** I'm not saying you can't pray about the mountain and talk to God about it, but eventually, He's going to ask you, *"Why don't you talk to it?"* The verse actually says, "For verily I say unto **you**, That **whosoever shall say** unto this mountain..."

What is a mountain? In this case, it was a real mountain. Remember the geography going from Bethany to Jerusalem? Jerusalem is built on Mount Zion. If you go down through the Valley of Kidron and up the other side, you'll come up on the Mount of Olives. Usually, the pictures you see of the City of Jerusalem, looking down over the Dome of the Rock or Temple Mount, are often taken from the Mount of Olives. I don't know which mountain Jesus was talking about; He's probably pointing at the Mount of Olives, Mount Zion, or one of these around there when He spoke to Peter.

This passage begins with Peter reminding Jesus about cursing the fig tree the day before.

> "And Peter calling to remembrance saith unto him, Master, behold, the fig tree which thou cursedst is withered away" (Mark 11:21).

Looking at the mountains, Jesus immediately takes His example further and answers them:

> And Jesus answering saith unto them, Have faith in God. **For verily I say unto you, That**

> **whosoever shall say unto this mountain,** Be
> thou removed, and be thou cast into the sea; and
> shall not doubt in his heart, but shall believe
> that those things which he saith shall come to
> pass; he shall have whatsoever he saith.
> Therefore I say unto you, What things soever
> ye desire, when ye pray, believe that ye receive
> them, and ye shall have them (Mark 11:22-24,
> emphasis added).

Jesus draws a comparison in size between the fig tree and the mountain. He contrasts the two, *"Oh, you think this fig tree is something, this is a tiny, miniscule thing in relation to what you are really capable of doing. This is just a small thing by comparison to what I've put in you."*

The Lord admonishes us, "Say unto this mountain, be thou removed and be thou cast into the sea." Then He adds, "… and shall not doubt in his heart" (Mark 11:23). This is where some people get into trouble. It does not say to tell the mountain, *"Mountain, come over here, stand as close to me as you can because I am going to dress and clean you up, making you look as good as possible. I'm going to take you with me wherever I go, so people will know I have a pet mountain."* That's the way we treat a lot of our troubles.

You may not know, but Christians have pet devils. When they don't want to get rid of one, people dress them up and take these pet devils with them. They make it religious and take it to church. They don't intend to quit anything to overcome it. They just paint it up, "religiousize" it, and take it with them wherever they go.

Ears to Hear

Mark chapter four comes into play here with Jesus teaching about the amount of thought and attention you give to God's Word—He that hath ears to hear, let him hear. Combine this with Proverbs' wisdom to protect your spirit—guard your spirit—at all costs, for out of it flows the issues of life. You must understand that what is in you is that which controls you. What is in you determines what your future is going to be.

Often, we **talk about** the mountain instead of **talking to** the mountain. We talk about our troubles, problems, woes, fears, and failures—everything except talking to the problem. Talking about how the situation is overwhelming and overtaking us is normal. We say how depressed we are and how we are going broke because of the problem. We talk about how the problem is killing us. We do everything but talk to the problem.

The mountain in your life could be the actual Mount of Olives or Mount Zion. However, you can't just tell a mountain to move unless you have heard from God because faith comes by hearing and hearing by the Word of God. You must have a word from God to speak to literal mountains. But you already have a word from God related to life's problems, difficulties, and challenges. Jesus called you to overcome. You don't have to have a special word from God to speak over your day-to-day routines; He has already given you the Bible.

God said He would make you the head and not the tail, above and not beneath. He will bless you going in and going out; the labor of your hand will be blessed and cause you to overcome. This is the victory that overcomes the world, even our faith. Whatsoever is born of God overcomes this world. He said all those glorious things so you could act on them. You are a world-overcomer and more than a conqueror, so get at it.

13
CONFESSING YOUR FAITH

When you speak to the mountain, the substance that works against it—that invisible spiritual Caterpillar™ bulldozer—is faith. That bulldozer of faith comes out and starts running up and down the side of that mountain—whuuump, vroooom, crash, rrroooar, whuuump, vroooom.

You go to bed and get up; you sleep and rise. Night and day, the seed springs forth and grows up, and you don't know how. That dozer is running up and down the side of that mountain for you as long as your confession stays right.

You might say, *"Well, that mountain will never move."* Guess what? Now the bulldozer of faith is back in the garage. The way you keep it out there working is by your confession. You keep it out there day and night, 24-7.

Applying Faith

The worlds were framed by the Word of God. We saw this in Genesis:

> In the beginning God created the heaven and
> the earth. And the earth was without form, and
> void; and darkness was upon the face of the
> deep. And the Spirit of God moved upon the
> face of the waters (Genesis 1:1-2).

I want you to notice that the Spirit of God moved upon the
face of the waters. The Spirit was present but not yet focused
on a mission; He was there to do the work.

Let's look at how this works. Do you remember in the book of
Luke where they let the guy down through the roof of the
house?

> And it came to pass on a certain day, as he was
> teaching, that there were Pharisees and doctors
> of the law sitting by, which were come out of
> every town of Galilee, and Judaea, and
> Jerusalem: and the power of the Lord was
> present to heal them. And, behold, men
> brought in a bed a man which was taken with a
> palsy: and they sought means to bring him in,
> and to lay him before him. And when they
> could not find by what way they might bring
> him in because of the multitude, they went
> upon the housetop, and let him down through
> the tiling with his couch into the midst before
> Jesus. And when he saw their faith, he said unto
> him, Man, thy sins are forgiven thee. And the
> scribes and the Pharisees began to reason,
> saying, Who is this which speaketh
> blasphemies? Who can forgive sins, but God

alone? But when Jesus perceived their thoughts, he answering said unto them, What reason ye in your hearts? Whether is easier, to say, Thy sins be forgiven thee; or to say, Rise up and walk? But that ye may know that the Son of man hath power upon earth to forgive sins, (he said unto the sick of the palsy,) I say unto thee, Arise, and take up thy couch, and go into thine house. And immediately he rose up before them, and took up that whereon he lay, and departed to his own house, glorifying God. And they were all amazed, and they glorified God, and were filled with fear, saying, We have seen strange things to day (Luke 5:17-26).

This event occurred after Jesus had already preached to the religious people. The Spirit of the Lord was present to heal, but no one was healed except that one man who came down through the ceiling. Even though the Spirit of God was present to heal the religious crowd, no one else was healed.

The Spirit of God can be present to do things but will not do anything until a command is given. So, the Spirit of the Lord moved upon the face of the waters, and then God spoke. God said. Uncle Roscoe didn't say it; God said it. Now, when God spoke, the Spirit of God went to work.

For those who have the faith of God or the God-kind of faith, we use our faith the same way God did. You have to **say** to the mountain, "Be thou removed." Then the bulldozer of faith comes out and...whuuump, whuuump, vroooom, craaash, whuuump, vroooom...up and down the mountain it goes.

You say, *"It's not working because I can't see any results."* The bulldozer goes back into the garage again. Then when you get your confession right again, the bulldozer comes out and starts working for you favorably.

My confession is that even in the worst economy—I don't know how, but it is assuredly guaranteed—this economic situation in the world today is working together for my good. Whuuump, whuuump, vroooom, craaash—my dozer is working on that mountain because I am keeping a right confession. I hope it's working for your good, too, but some people keep putting the dozer back in the garage.

Pull the bulldozer out of the garage and start it by applying faith to the problem—faith to the mountain. You use it properly like Jesus, the author and finisher of that faith, skillfully uses His tools. The more precise you are in the use of the unseen substance will determine the results you get from it.

The amount of attention, thought, and understanding you give to the Word determines what it gives back to you. If you are casual about it, you'll get casual results. If you are precise with it; you'll get precise results.

Framing Your Confession

Look in Genesis:

> And God said, Let there be light: and there was light. And God saw the light, that it was good:...The evening and the morning were the first day...And God said, Let the waters

under the heaven be gathered together...
(Genesis 1:3-5, 9).

People want to argue and say, *"Well, God could not have used faith to create because that would imply God had to put faith in a higher being than Himself. Since He is the ultimate being, the highest of all beings, God could not have used faith to create the world."* Hebrews 11:3 stands in the way of that line of thought which says, "Through faith we understand that the worlds were framed by the word of God." In other words: we understand that through faith, the worlds were framed. That's the best way to translate that verse.

So, we understand that the worlds were formed and framed. God envisions what He wants to create. Like an artist who takes a brush and creates an image on the canvas, stroke by stroke, line by line, precisely. The better the artist, the more valuable the painting. For example, an original Rembrandt, Gauguin, or Monet is a little more valuable than my Uncle Joe's original, even though his kids may argue the point.

We read in Genesis that the worlds were framed by the Word of God. God took his paintbrush and loaded it up with a substance called faith. He moved it all around, forming and framing the worlds with it, but that faith is invisible. However, it becomes visible when coupled with the confession of someone who believes in it. That invisible thing that sits on the shelf of the spirit is called faith, and when it is connected with the confession from the mouth of a person who believes it, it then becomes visible. This is the visible substance of things hoped for—the visible evidence of things not seen. You take the unseen and make it seen by using the words of your mouth. That is exactly how you do it; it doesn't happen any other way.

Someone says, *"Well, I'm going to ask God to do it."* That's all well and good, but God gave you the spirit of faith and a mouth.

How to Use Your Faith

Here's what the Bible says about when God first created man:

> And God said, Let us make man in our image, after our likeness: and let them have dominion over the fish of the sea, and over the fowl of the air, and over the cattle, and over all the earth, and over every creeping thing that creepeth upon the earth (Genesis 1:26).

Chapter two of Genesis gives us a **re-creation of man**, and it says that God breathed into man the breath of life (Genesis 2:7). There is an interpretation that says it this way, "God breathed into man and made man a speaking spirit." God breathed the breath of life into you; He didn't give other animals the power to speak. Now, you may love your dog, but your dog can't talk. I don't care what Scooby says on the Cartoon Network®; it's not happening. They do not have the power to say anything; therefore, they do not have the ability to use faith.

When the Bible says we are created in the image of God, it does not simply mean that we look like Him; it means we act like Him—it means that we have an anointing and authority. Christians don't have God's authority, but we do have the authority He gave us. For example, I don't have the authority to create **the** worlds, but I do have the authority to create **my** world.

An example of different worlds that I'm sure you'll remember is from the Christmas story. A decree went out from Caesar Augustus that all the world should be taxed. However, the world that was taxed did not include everyone in the world. Instead, it was the world Caesar Augustus had influence over. A world can be where you influence, not the entire world. Your world. Your faith is the victory that overcomes your world.

An example of the operation of faith can be found by looking at the story of Elisha and the Shunammite woman:

> And it fell on a day, that Elisha passed to Shunem, where was a great woman; and she constrained him to eat bread. And so it was, that as oft as he passed by, he turned in thither to eat bread. And she said unto her husband, Behold now, I perceive that this is an holy man of God, which passeth by us continually (2 Kings 4:8-9).

If you will remember, this woman built an addition to her house for the prophet to stay. She was evidently a woman of some substance.

> And [Elisha] said unto [Gehazi], **Say now unto her, Behold, thou hast been careful for us with all this care; what is to be done for thee?** wouldest thou be spoken for to the king, or to the captain of the host? And she answered, I dwell among mine own people (2 Kings 4:13, emphasis added).

Elisha commended the woman by saying, "...Behold, thou hast been careful for us..." So, he asked Gehazi, his assistant, *"What does this woman want? What does she need?"* In other words, Elisha was saying, *"You have taken diligent care of us with all this attention. What is to be done for you? What do you want?"* A prophet had the right to ask because they had prominence, stature, and political influence in those days. They were not just some preachers down on the corner.

Elisha asked the woman, *"Do you want me to get your tax burden removed?"* Think if someone said that to you today. *"Do you want to live the rest of your life without paying taxes?"* You would certainly say, "Yes!" That would be a good raise, wouldn't it?

Gehazi tells Elisha, "Verily, she has no child and her husband is old" (2 Kings 4:14). Elisha's response to this reveals that she is going to have a son, and she did. That child was the prophet's reward.

Later, we see where the child becomes ill:

> And when the child was grown, it fell on a day,
> that he went out to his father to the reapers.
> And he said unto his father, My head, my head.
> And he said to a lad, Carry him to his mother (2
> Kings 4:18-19).

Long story short, the child died. You see the mother's response to her child's death at the end of verse 22:

> And she called unto her husband, and said,
> Send me, I pray thee, one of the young men,
> and one of the asses, that I may run to the man
> of God, and come again (2 Kings 4:22).

In other words, she's saying, *"I'm going to run to God with this child He gave me."* Do you understand the crisis that this woman is in? Look at verse twenty-three:

> And [her husband] said, Wherefore wilt thou go to him to day? it is neither new moon, nor sabbath. And she said, It shall be well (2 Kings 4:23).

Do you know what she didn't say? She didn't say, *"Good Lord, this is a disaster!"* When you don't know what else to say, you can say, *"It shall be well."* When you're in the middle of a crisis, jammed in a corner, and you don't know what else to do— when it looks like all hell is coming against you, and every bad thing known to man is standing against you, you know what you need to say? You need to say, *"It is well."*

If you want to change things and turn them to your good, you need to watch what you do and then watch how you come out of this. The Shunammite woman "saddled an ass, and said to her servant, Drive, and go forward..." (2 Kings 4:24).

Let's look at the next verses:

> The man of God saw her afar off, that he said to Gehazi his servant, Behold, yonder is that Shunammite: Run now, I pray thee, to meet her, and say unto her, Is it well with thee? is it well with thy husband? is it well with the child? And she answered, It is well (2 Kings 4:25b-26).

Did you notice their questions? What was her answer? Did she say, *"Oh, my God, if you don't get there before morning— it's awful.*

I don't know what we're gonna do. My God! I thought God loved me, and I thought God wanted to help me"? No, she didn't say those things.

What do you do when the doctor gives you a bad report? Do you fall apart, or do you get it under control? I hope you understand that this is serious stuff! You can have what you say. So, speak to the mountain: be thou removed and be thou cast into the sea, and it will obey you.

In the beginning, God said let there be light, and there was light. We understand that by the words God released, He framed the worlds. What world are you getting ready to frame? What world was this Shunammite woman getting ready to frame? She could have changed everything right there at that moment; she could have framed a different world.

> And he went up, and lay upon the child, and put his mouth upon his mouth, and his eyes upon his eyes, and his hands upon his hands: and stretched himself upon the child; and the flesh of the child waxed warm. Then he returned, and walked in the house to and fro; and went up, and stretched himself upon him: and the child sneezed seven times, and the child opened his eyes. And he called Gehazi, and said, Call this Shunammite. So he called her. And when she was come in unto him, he said, Take up thy son (2 Kings 4:34-36).

Now, if the Shunammite woman had said, *"It is bad,"* she would not have made it to this point.

"Then she went in, and fell at his feet, and bowed herself to the ground, and took up her son, and went out" (2 Kings 4:37).

Now, there are times when you get a lot of bad news, so you better put a clamp on your mouth—and you better do it immediately. When that doctor comes out and tells you what you don't want to hear, you better put a clamp on it immediately.

If you have nothing to say, just say, *"I don't know how, but it is well."* Doing that is not ignoring things. It is taking your faith and using it like a carpenter uses a tool, like an artist uses a brush, and saying what you need to say to get the results you need to get.

What do you say when you get a pink slip at work? *"It is well."* What if you get a notification that you are part of the layoff? That doesn't change anything. God was my source when I came here, and God will be my source when I leave. Just courteously stand and walk out.

You might want to prepare ahead for those critical moments when you don't have time to prepare—when you don't have time to rehearse the answer. We are either going to fail at this thing, or we're going to win. It's our choice.

> Take your faith and use it like a carpenter uses a tool or an artist uses a brush, and say what you need to say to get the results you want.

14
ACTING RIGHT

Have you ever known you were going into a potentially confrontational setting? Maybe you are going to have a conversation that you really don't want to have. The best thing you can do is rehearse your answers before you go. Calm yourself inside; calm your spirit. Determine that you're not going to blurt out something stupid. Decide that you're not going to be provoked. Determine your answers to obvious questions. Ask yourself certain questions, and then give yourself a predetermined, canned response. Get it under control. Know what you are going to say. Gain the confidence you need to stay above the provocation, temper, anger impulses, and unchecked emotions. Say the right things. Do the right things. Act the right way.

We have too many examples of yelling heads—not talking heads—on television. We have a news media panel discussion where it seems like the one who gets the loudest wins. And then the same four people come back tomorrow and do it again. After it's all said and done, they will all go out to dinner together. They are not mad at each other; it's just good TV.

But you see, we get provoked by an issue and feel compelled to offer a response analogous to another's statement. We somehow feel obliged to get all worked up like the yelling heads; it becomes compulsory to yell. The proper response is to rant, rave, and scream. But, no! We must get it under control; we don't have to react. Just give a canned response. Condition yourself by working through scenarios.

What would happen if I did get laid off? What would my response be? You might say something like, *"It's been nice working here. I've enjoyed it, and I'm thankful for it. However, the same God that brought me here is the same God that will take me to my next level. It is well because my God meets my needs according to His riches in glory by Christ Jesus."* **That** is my confession, and there is no other. At that point, something changes, and something begins to switch. Something good starts to turn in your direction.

Some might ask, *"Well, what are we going to do if the economy fails?"* Please understand that heaven's economy has never failed, and I live in a heavenly kingdom. I live based on the supply from heaven. The same God who met the needs of the children of Israel in the wilderness—the same God who opened the manna ovens in heaven—is the same God that I am in covenant with, and He is the same God that meets my needs today. So we don't have to panic. It is well. That is a great truth!

In the middle of crises, turmoil, and difficulties—in the middle of all hell breaking loose—a person who can control their spirit says, *"It is well."* The Bible says one who can rule their spirit is greater than he who can take a city (Proverbs 16:32). When you can act like that in the middle of everything that looks contrary, you are going to win at life.

Panic is never the will of God.

But, if you fly apart like a two-dollar watch, you will lose. Panic is never the will of God. Fear and faith do not work together; when fear takes over, faith leaves the room. The devil's tactic is to use fear to shock you into saying something he can use against you. He wants to terrorize you so he can scare you into something to take control of your future. So, you blurt out some unbelief, followed by, *"I didn't mean it."* The devil doesn't care whether you meant it or not; meaning it has nothing to do with it. It's the act of using words, even when you don't feel like they're the right words, that will seal your future.

Someone may believe, *"You have to feel it before you say it. I just say what I feel."* It is foolish to say whatever you feel. You don't want to do that. Another might say, *"I just say what I think."* Well, I hope you like your life.

Refrain from Evil

> "For he that will love life, and see good days, let him refrain his tongue from evil, and his lips that they speak no guile" (1 Peter 3:10).

Do you love life? If you love life and want to see good days, Peter is going to tell you the formula for getting it: "Let him refrain his tongue from evil."

Evil is not just using inappropriate or vulgar words; it is using words that are contrary to God. Do you remember those spies that went in and reconnoitered the Promised Land? The Bible says they came back and talked to the congregation—the nation of Israel—about how they could not go on and how they would be overcome. They said things like, *"We are nothing but*

SPEAKING FAITH-FILLED WORDS

grasshoppers in the full scheme of things. There are giants in the land. It is a land that flows with milk and honey, but we cannot tap into it." The Bible called this an evil report.

An evil report is not merely going around saying bad words. That would be one definition of it, but let's look further.

If you want to have a good life and enjoy the life you have, watch what you say. What is cursing? In the South, we call it "cussing." You may hear someone cursing—blankety-blank this, blankety-blank that—but that's not the only words we say that are evil. There are many things that are evil.

Again, 1 Peter 3:10 says to let him refrain his tongue from evil and his lips from speaking guile. Guile is deceit—making up stories and trying to bring harm to another person. You may not use *"God #%&@"* in a sentence, but that might be the result of what you want to happen. You may want God to do it to them.

Speaking guile is not necessarily that blatant—it's when you have a deceptive motive. You remember what Jesus said about Nathanael: He said to behold a man in whom there is no guile. In other words, He said, *"Concerning this man, what you see is truly what you get; this man does not have an ulterior motive. He does not think one thing and say something else to you."*

> As he loved cursing, so let it come unto him: as he delighted not in blessing, so let it be far from him. As he clothed himself with cursing like as with his garment, so let it come into his bowels like water, and like oil into his bones (Psalm 109:17-18).

In other words, God is saying that for people who curse, what they say comes back on them. Is that what you want in your life? Some think, *"Well, that won't come to me."* That's not what the Bible says IF you are going to live according to the Bible. The person in Psalm 109 wouldn't speak a blessing; he'd rather speak curses. For that man, the Bible says the blessing is far from him.

The blessing of God will walk away from a person who uses their words wrongfully. If you want God's blessing on your life, you must speak correctly. God says that you have been blessed with faithful Abraham, and the blessing of Abraham is on you through Christ Jesus. God wants to bless you. He's given you a blessing, but you can't have that blessing unless your words are used correctly.

Notice that Psalm 109:18 says, "As he clothed himself with cursing…" A coat is clothing that I put on to wear. When you look at me, you see more of the coat than you see of me, but this coat is not me; I only wear it. The blessing is not you; the blessing is worn by you. **The blessing becomes visible on you when your words are right.**

You cannot talk poverty and have abundance. You cannot talk depression and have peace. You must speak what you want. You must talk about blessing and favor. The passage in Psalm 109 continues:

> As he clothed himself with cursing like as with his garment, so let it come into his bowels like water, and like oil into his bones. Let it be unto him as the garment which covereth him, and for a girdle wherewith he is girded continually. Let

this be the reward of mine adversaries from the Lord, and of them that speak evil against my soul (Psalm 109:18-20).

God says if you use your mouth as a tool for cursing, you will have to wear it like a blanket. You might be saying, "GD this, GD that, and GD them," but God said, that's your curse. You put curses out there rather than blessing them; now you are going to wear them. Ouch! That should be enough to sweeten our vocabularies.

God is saying: if you want to have a good life, refrain your tongue from evil and your lips so that they speak no guile. This is the power of speaking faith-filled words. It's a powerful thing.

A Prayerful Confession of Faith

Lord, put a watch over our mouths that we speak the right way, that we get better at saying the right things. We want to do this better and more properly. We are going to say the right things and not just blurt out something. We will use our words like the pen of a ready writer. We are going to indite a good matter. We are going to speak of a future that has a blessing on it.

Lord, you said when we speak a curse, we wear it like a coat. Well, Lord, if we wear a curse like a coat, we can wear a blessing like one as well. So, Lord, we speak blessings.

We walk in the blessing of the Most High God because we're His children. We are the head and not the tail, above and not beneath. We are highly, highly favored of the Lord.

Lord, we don't just say these things to be saying them; we say them because You said them. And so, Lord, that is what we are going to walk in. That is what we will have. Put a watch over our mouths so we do not sin against you in these areas. Lord, we thank you and give you praise for it, in Jesus' name.

SPEAKING FAITH-FILLED WORDS

15
GOD GOES BEFORE YOU

A serious event happened in the apostle Paul's life while he was on his way to Rome. The ship he was sailing on was involved in a massive storm—a hurricane, cyclone, or typhoon. During the trip, Paul perceived a warning that there would be some danger on the voyage, and he told the crew. Then, following the storm, Paul admonished them that they should have listened:

> But after long abstinence Paul stood forth in the midst of them, and said, Sirs, ye should have hearkened unto me, and not have loosed from Crete, and to have gained this harm and loss (Acts 27:21).

God was ahead of the storm and gave Paul a witness of the Spirit; he announced to his shipmates, *"The ship is going down, but there will be no loss of life."* He told them to be of good cheer—he had heard from God:

> And now I exhort you to be of good cheer: for there shall be no loss of any man's life among you, but of the ship. For there stood by me this

night the angel of God, whose I am, and whom
I serve (Acts 27:22-23).

If you study the Bible, you will find distinguishing descriptions
of angels, not just a single generic one. According to this verse,
the angel mentioned here is **the angel of God.** All angels, apart
from the fallen, are angels of God; they are all under His orders.
However, the Bible also talks about "the angel of the Lord." In
addition, angels sent to the Church at Ephesus and the Church
of Thyatira are referred to differently.

In this situation, we don't just see an angel of God, but **the
angel of God**. There is a point of reference here that is
important to underscore in your thinking that this angel has a
unique position with extraordinary power, and I would
certainly imagine this angel also had an exceptional assignment.
Paul continued by saying:

> For there stood by me this night the angel of
> God, whose I am, and whom I serve, Saying,
> Fear not, Paul; thou must be brought before
> Caesar: and, lo, God hath given thee all them
> that sail with thee. Wherefore, sirs, be of good
> cheer: for I believe God, that it shall be even as
> it was told me (Acts 27:23-25).

God went before the storm, and this passage says He had
already given Paul all those who sailed with him. These people
did not have a covenant with the Lord; they were heathen
sailors just doing a job.

At this time, the Church was extremely young, and Paul was being sent to Rome on assignment by the Lord. No matter what it looks like, they may have him chained, but he is actually being sent to Rome by God. I have little doubt that this storm was sent to confuse the issue by taking Paul out of commission if the devil could get by with it. The devil didn't care about the others in the boat; they just happened to be tools or pawns. This storm was not sent for their benefit; they were nothing to him. The storm's presence was all about sending Paul to the bottom of the sea—killing him. Sometimes, people get caught up in things—not necessarily because they are the target, but because they are secondary to the mission. However, there still was this word from the Lord to Paul saying, *"Because of you, I'm going to deliver all these people sailing with you."* That assurance came from the angel of God.

Another example of God going before us is found in the story of Isaac:

> And he said unto me, The Lord, before whom I walk, will send **his angel** with thee, and prosper thy way; and thou shalt take a wife for my son [Isaac] of my kindred, and of my father's house (Genesis 24:40, emphasis added).

In this case, the assignment was to find a wife for Isaac. The servant's way prospered, being able to find the right wife. His blessing was due to an angel being sent before him to prosper his way.

When It Looks Bad

"For he that will love life, and see good days, let him
refrain his tongue from evil, and his lips that they
speak no guile" (1 Peter 3:10).

Everyone wants to love life and see good days! Yet, even during
hard times, we can be assured that God has gone before us
when we speak faith-filled words. Let's look at that in the
Amplified Bible:

> For let him who wants to enjoy life and see good
> days [good—whether apparent or not] keep his
> tongue free from evil and his lips from guile
> (treachery, deceit) (1 Peter 3:10, AMPC).

There are times in life when things will happen that don't
appear to be good at first, but they turn out to be good in the
end. God is working on a plan you don't always see.

Sometimes you think something would be the worst thing in
the world, but God sees the end from the beginning the whole
time. He has already gone before you and knows things you
don't know. Because God has gone before you, all things are
working together for the good of those who love Him and are
called according to His purpose—even though you think it's
not working in your favor. For some, this truth has been used
as a cliché or catchphrase, but the truth of the matter is that
God is shaping and molding all things together for your good.
God has a good plan for you. He has a good strategy for your
life. Even though it doesn't always appear that way, He's
working in your favor.

16

POWER OF FAITH-FILLED WORDS

The Bible tells us that what you say is important; your words are important. The emphasis of what we are talking about is faith-filled words. In the verses below, your **belly** is the innermost part of your being. We see here that we have the power to control certain things.

Death and Poverty

> A man's belly shall be satisfied with the fruit of his mouth; and with the increase of his lips shall he be filled. Death and life are in the power of the tongue: and they that love it shall eat the fruit thereof (Proverbs 18:20-21).

When talking about death, we often have this small definition of what it is. Sometimes death is defined as the end of this life as we know it. When the physical body ceases to function and we transition on into that next life, we often refer to it as death.

However, death is more of a person or a being than just an event. Satan is the author of all death; death came from him.

Death came by sin, which is connected to the work of the devil or the works of darkness.

There are many expressions of death that are not necessarily just the cessation of life. Anything that negatively produces is an expression of death. All negativity is death. Sickness is an expression of death—not a full manifestation, but an expression of it, nonetheless.

Poverty is also an expression of death. Some people take issue with whether the Bible teaches poverty or prosperity. Some say that the Bible doesn't really teach prosperity. But, I can assure you, the only person who would say that is someone who has never been where poverty rules the day. If you see where poverty rules, you will know there is no virtue in it—what the full manifestation of it does to human beings: starvation, malnutrition, sickness, disease, and loss of human dignity. When you see all that, you must know that it cannot be sent from God.

A person might say, *"Well, I don't know about that, but I don't believe this prosperity message."* What they are saying is that they don't believe greed is right. Greed and prosperity are not the same. If we believe that prosperity is just giving us stuff so we can have more, we are wrong; that is not prosperity; that is greed.

God's Prosperity

Prosperity is walking in the blessing of the Lord; it's walking in God's favor and receiving from heaven the things heaven desires for you. Sometimes people get their wording wrong and get turned off by it, or we get an aversion to something the Lord wants to say to us because we see excess and greed. God's not in favor of all kinds of abuse and misuse. People get the wrong idea that this is the prosperity message, but it's not. **The prosperity message is walking in the favor of the Lord and walking in His blessing.** That is the prosperity message.

Some things accompany God's prosperity, but there are times that God may ask you to give up what the world calls prosperity in favor of a better walk with Him. He told Abraham to come out from among his family and friends and go another way. Sometimes you will not go in the same direction as the money. Prosperity is not just about money; it's about a plethora of other things as well.

Bridling the Tongue

We are talking about speaking and releasing faith-filled words—the power of faith-filled words.

> Not many [of you] should become teachers (self-constituted censors and reprovers of others), my brethren, for you know that we [teachers] will be judged by a higher standard and with greater severity [than other people; thus we assume the greater accountability and the more condemnation] (James 3:1, AMPC).

In other words, God is saying to teachers in the Body of Christ that they have a higher responsibility. So you better be sure what you teach is right; you don't need to be misleading people.

Verse two goes on to say, "For in many things we offend all…" (James 3:2). It almost seems like there's a transition in these verses. You might think you can start in verse two without reading verse one, but there is a reason the Holy Spirit put those two verses together. I have found that what people are taught is the determining factor of what they do to a great extent. There are some people who can stand on their own two feet and reject wrong teaching, but for many, they will walk in a negative way if they hear a great deal of bad teaching.

This verse continues about the role of the teacher: "For in many things we offend all. If any man offend not in word, the same is a perfect man, and able also to bridle the whole body" (James 3:2).

Let's look at verse two in the Amplified Classic Version. Don't read it with your religious glasses on; read it like it means what it says:

> For we all often stumble and fall and offend in
> many things. And if anyone does not offend in
> speech [never says the wrong things], he is a
> fully developed character and a perfect man,
> able to control his whole body and to curb his
> entire nature (James 3:2, AMPC).

The Bible says that your body—your human nature and all the things related to it—can give you a fit on this earth. We all know that's true. Christians are to control our flesh, which is comprised of the **soma** (or body) and **sarx**, which is your fleshly nature. Getting those two things under control is the key to being a successful Christian—not just as a Christian, but life in general. Do you understand what that verse just said to you?

The Bible says that if you can get your words under control, you can bridle your body.

Someone might say, *"I just can't get my body under control."* You are right about that because your words won't let you; they are working against you. Your words must begin to form what you want your body to do before your body will do it.

"But, I just can't seem to read my Bible." Well, change your words, and the body will begin to follow. *"I just don't want to pray."* You need to change what you're saying about your "want-to." If you do not want to pray, ask God to give you the "want-to." Start where you are by saying something like, *"God, please put a hunger in me."* Then start to agree with what you pray and talk about to God. Don't let your body tell you what you want to do. You can't just let your mouth run amok.

Controlling Your Flesh

If you often say, *"I just can't seem to get my temper under control,"* look at this potent passage:

> Even so the tongue is a little member, and boasteth great things. Behold, how great a matter a little fire kindleth! And the tongue is a fire, a world of iniquity: so is the tongue among our members, that it defileth the whole body, and setteth on fire the course of nature; and it is set on fire of hell (James 3:5-6).

Your tongue is a little member of your body; it doesn't have to be significant. This passage indicates that your tongue can be extremely hot, which can start a fire going. The Bible says that your tongue can defile your whole body.

The tongue sets on fire the course of nature. When you see the word **"nature,"** there are many things to consider. You can think about nature as in Mother Nature; however, this passage is not talking about nature in that regard. It means the human nature—your internal nature—who you are.

"A short fuse is my nature," you say. Oh, really? The Bible says your tongue sets on fire the course of your nature. You cannot get that temper under control until you get your tongue under control. The longer you say that you can't control it, the longer you'll stay out of control. Start to reverse its control by changing your confession concerning life. Life and death are in the power of the tongue. If you want to, you can put what is besetting you to death by the words of your mouth.

Let's focus on verse six in the Amplified:

> And the tongue is a fire. [The tongue is a] world of wickedness set among our members, contaminating and depraving the whole body and setting on fire the wheel of birth (the cycle of man's nature), being itself ignited by hell (Gehenna) (James 3:6, AMPC).

This verse talks about how the words of your mouth can defile your whole body. Hell is targeting your tongue because the devil wants to control it. You must understand something about the devil: he has virtually zero power in this earth unless he uses a human to make it happen. The devil is a creature without a body but needs one to do his work. He must get you to do what he wants in order to enforce his will and have his way in the earth. So, the devil shoots at your tongue to get you to say what he wants you to say.

Someone says, *"Well, this is just killing me."* There you go; your tongue just got shot at, and you took the bait. Do you really want it to kill you? Is that your desire? If you don't mean it, then don't say it because in doing so, you set in motion the laws that govern it. Your body is controlled by your words. Speak what you want to happen.

Sadly, some testify by saying, *"I'm dying from cancer."* If you're not at the point of getting rid of cancer by what you say, at least begin to say that you're living with it. Start where you are. You are not dead yet, or else you wouldn't be reading this today. You must begin to say what you want to happen.

Don't talk about how you can't ever get your temper under control or how you can't exercise. By doing so, you set in motion the course of your life. Let's look at that same verse in a couple of other translations:

> And the tongue is a fire, a world of iniquity; the tongue is set among our members as that which defiles the entire body, and sets on fire the course of our life, and is set on fire by hell (James 3:6, NASB).

> The tongue also is a fire, a world of evil among the parts of the body. It corrupts the whole body (person), sets the whole course of one's life on fire, and is itself set on fire by hell (James 3:6, NIV).

The entire course of your life is determined by what you say. You can't even get saved without saying it. The Bible teaches that the more you talk about the Lord, the bigger He grows in your life. It's so important that there is an archive in heaven that records what you say.

It doesn't make any difference if you want to speak correctly or not because you are still controlled by what you say. Even if you don't want to hear teaching on this particular subject—it doesn't matter if you listen to it or not; you are still doing it. The point is not if you will be controlled by your words; they are controlling you. It is not whether you are going to continue doing it; **you are going to continue**. As long as you live, you're going to do this. It is just whether you're working it in your favor or whether you're working it against you. Whether you do it favorably or sit on your hands and let it turn out unfavorably. The Bible says that your nature is set on fire by your tongue. Not only that, but the words of your mouth also control the course of your life. You are going to get out of this life what you say. Therefore, the power of speaking faith-filled words is critical.

17

TAKE NO THOUGHT

And why **take ye thought** for raiment? Consider the lilies of the field, how they grow; they toil not, neither do they spin: And yet I say unto you, That even Solomon in all his glory was not arrayed like one of these. Wherefore, if God so clothe the grass of the field, which to day is, and to morrow is cast into the oven, shall he not much more clothe you, O ye of little faith? Therefore **take no thought, saying**, What shall we eat? or, What shall we drink? or, Wherewithal shall we be clothed? (For after all these things do the Gentiles seek:) for your heavenly Father knoweth that ye have need of all these things. But seek ye first the kingdom of God, and his righteousness; and all these things shall be added unto you. **Take therefore no thought** for the morrow: for the morrow shall take thought for the things of itself. Sufficient unto the day is the evil thereof (Matthew 6:28-34, emphasis added).

This passage is talking about all the thoughts that flow by or that you reach up and grab. For example, if you are going to catch a baseball, you better put on a mitt. That baseball is hard and painful to catch bare-handed; put on a glove if you want to do it. Put on the mitt, reach out, and catch the ball.

In the same way, there are thoughts that come; the room where you are sitting right now is full of words—all kinds of words, music, and images flowing through the room. There are broadcast towers in every city sending out signals all day, every day. With the proper equipment (with the right mitt), you can reach out and catch a signal. You can also reach out and connect with someone preaching the good Word of God or someone giving you the latest news, pitching you a car or new gutters. If you use the right machine, with the right antenna, on the correct frequency, and hook it all up properly, the signal comes through. You can catch the signals that are out there.

We didn't always have that equipment at our disposal; it did not exist. But now, technology has progressed to the point where catching those signals has become commonplace. There are towers and satellites used to send out AM and FM radio, television, GPS coordinates, internet access, and other signals all the time. As a result, you can hear all kinds of voices talking to you as they constantly flow through. Just turn on your receiver of choice, and you'll hear them. Get the right receiver with the right set of circumstances, and you can catch the signal.

In addition to these signals, there are thoughts flowing through the atmosphere all the time. Thoughts are eternal. Thoughts convey. You can send thoughts. Thoughts and words carry. So, we send thoughts, and we do it by words. The Bible instructs us when it says, "take no thought saying." You take thoughts by saying them.

With all these thoughts coming through—flowing at you, you need to reach out and catch the right ones. You cannot stop thoughts from flowing, not even the negative ones, but you don't have to reach out and grab one. When someone says you can't do something or when a person tells you that you're going to fail miserably, you don't have to stretch out and catch that one. You can't prevent thoughts from flowing across or those words from streaming through any more than you can stop TV and radio signals from flowing through a room. Instead, give your attention to other words in the atmosphere.

If you don't know how to receive them, or you don't know how to pick them up, just get your Bible out and read some of those. Many good promises have been written down, and you can put them in your mouth. However, if you don't want a thought, turn the receiver off. If thoughts or words are inconsistent with what you believe for your future, then turn off the equipment. Turn off the radio, television, phone, tablet, or computer. You don't have to **take** every thought that smacks you in the back of the head. **The Bible says we take a thought by saying it; you don't take a thought by thinking it.**

If You Think It, You Will Speak It

If you think a thought long enough, you will say it. The Bible teaches, "...for out of the abundance of the heart the mouth speaketh" (Matthew 12:34). This truth is also found in the book of Luke:

> A good man out of the good treasure of his
> heart bringeth forth that which is good; and an
> evil man out of the evil treasure of his heart

bringeth forth that which is evil: **for of the abundance of the heart his mouth speaketh** (Luke 6:45, emphasis added).

If you meditate on anything for an extended period of time, you will speak it. You will begin to say what you see and think. Once you start to say it, it begins to set the course for your life. It begins to shape your future.

A Small Rudder

> We can make a large horse turn around and go wherever we want by means of a small bit in his mouth. And a tiny rudder makes a huge ship turn wherever the pilot wants it to go, even though the winds are strong (James 3:3-4, TLB).

In other words, the captain controls the ship through this small thing on the stern called a rudder. You cannot turn a ship by getting in the water and pushing, nor can you swim in front of it and chart its course. These verses emphasize that you do not have the strength to control the course and future of your life on your own.

God is telling us that our tongues set the course for our future and are precisely like the horse's bit and the ship's rudder. Your future is decided by the words of your mouth. You need to ask yourself where you want to go.

A person might say, *"It doesn't matter. I grew up in a poor family from the wrong side of the tracks. Nothing ever happens good for me."* Think hard. Is that the course you want your life to take?

Is that the way you want it to go? Seriously, you are the determining factor in this. The power of life and death is in your tongue. There is only so much that you can be taught because at the end of the day, in the dark wee hours of the morning when no one's around, it's you who determines what you are going to say.

Every time you ask me, I'm going to tell you: I don't believe I'm poor, and I never will be poor. Some ask me, *"How can you conceivably say that?"* Well, it was easy. How do you say you will always be poor? You don't know the future any more than I do. How come it's so easy to say the negative, but people look at you cross-eyed if you say the positive? The reason is that we are geared to the negative and have been for so long that it doesn't even sound bad.

Your Confession in Troubled Times

I was at the gym recently, and a news report came up on the television in the locker room. Another man in there was offering up his commentary with colorful descriptive words, wanting me to agree with him about how unwise politicians are. My problem was I didn't have a broadcast delay circuit like TV stations have, so it all got through! He called these people "idiots" and even more colorful things, and then he'd just look at me, assuming that I agreed.

The next thing I know, this guy was telling me what these "idiots" were going to be able to do to me. Wrong, wrong, wrong. These politicians are probably unwise and have presumably made some bad decisions, but they are not running my future. I have a higher source, and there is a higher power responsible for my future than them. At the end of the day, I don't know how God's going to work things for me favorably, but He will. I'm coming out of this thing on top. I'm not coming out on the bottom—above only and not beneath, and you can do that, too.

Someone could say, *"What are you going to do now that all your retirement is lost?"* First, it's not lost till I say it's lost. *"Well, aren't you nervous because of all the money you've lost in this market downturn?"* No, because I have not lost it yet; it's not lost till I say it's lost. Now is the time to confess: I have a paid-up retirement; I have ample money to do what I am going to do. I have more than enough for my future. My God meets my need according to His riches in glory by Christ Jesus. I am here to tell you right now, that it's not lost. Why do you want to give it up so easily?

Someone may think that I'm just being Pollyanna about this. No, I am being faith-oriented. The Bible says the just shall live by faith, which means the unjust shall die without it. Choose which one you want to be. Let me tell you something: God can do it by hook or crook. It makes no difference how God has to do it; He will act on what you say when you speak according to the Bible.

God will multiply for you—look at the loaves and the fishes. Everyone did not get to eat that day, but all those who sat down and received did eat. In John 6, Jesus blessed that little boy's lunch and put it in the disciples' hands. The bread didn't multiply until the disciples gave it out. What's in your hands? God's hands without your hands will not work. God must get your hands involved before it is going to feed the multitude. So, put your hands in, and He will start multiplying. God is saying to us that our words are critical to our future.

18

CHANGE THAT LASTS

In this day and hour, you constantly need to use your faith. We all need to be taught and reminded. It doesn't make any difference if you've heard these truths 10,000 times; you still need to hear them again. We need to be reminded. It's not repetition for repetition's sake, but these things can slip from us if we're not careful to remind ourselves of them.

The Bible says:

> **This book of the law shall not depart out of thy mouth;** but thou shalt **meditate** therein day and night, that thou mayest observe to do according to all that is written therein: for then thou shalt make thy way prosperous, and then thou shalt have good success (Joshua 1:8, emphasis added).

Put in the Effort

When we are talking about the power of your words, the word "meditate" is crucial. Your words are critical because they will control your attitude and what you think about a situation—whether you believe you can come out on top or not. It is vital to remember that **I am** always comes before **I can**. If you don't believe you're smart, you won't even try. If you don't believe you're capable, you'll never put forth the effort. I am capable, so, therefore, I can do it.

Recently, I was flipping through the channels and saw a minute of a video vignette about the retired professional basketball legend Charles Barkley. As they interviewed him—"The Round Mound of Rebound," as he was called at Auburn University—he said basketball became important to him as a kid because it kept him from doing some things he knew he shouldn't do. Surprisingly, when Barkley started playing, he was not very good. Here is a guy whose name is a household word—one of the greatest of all time and a public favorite—who was not good when he first started. Still, he stayed with it and obviously became something special.

We hang these little clichés on our walls that say, "Anything worth doing is worth doing well." I'm sure that you've heard that a million times over the course of your life. However, the truth is: **anything worth doing is worth doing poorly** because before you do it well, you will do it poorly. If something is worth doing, you'll have to do it poorly at first because when you start, you don't know how to do it.

You will have to start doing things when it's not natural for you. You will have to start doing things when it seems abnormal, out of character, or difficult. We tend to gravitate toward the easy way, the natural way, and the way we have done it in the past; therefore, we'll do it the same way in the future. In this case, what happens is you leave the undiscovered still undiscovered. You never attempt to try something new.

For example, if you are going to be a good student, you must learn some effective study habits. In the beginning, you will not do it as well as you will later. Once you learn good study habits, the work may get more difficult, but it's not as hard as it was in the beginning because you know how to do it. You discipline yourself to be able to do it.

When I first began studying the Bible, it seemed a daunting task. It seemed so vast that I wondered how I would ever learn it all—I still don't know it all. At the time, it seemed so broad and immeasurable. Why would I ever start because I'll never complete it? But, I determined that I would apply myself to learning God's Word. Then God began to speak to me and show me things. As I continued to apply myself, He continued to show me things. After a while, I accumulated enough knowledge that I was no longer a baby. God said to desire the sincere milk of the Word that you may grow thereby. You start out as an infant, but then you grow up.

If you don't believe there's anything worth doing, you won't even try. If you don't believe you have any ability, you'll never start. You must begin to speak out what you want according to God's Word before seeing any evidence of it. You must set the course for your future in motion, beginning with talking to your mind. Then, you speak to your body and get it under control.

Turn off the television and study. You have a great deal of potential. Your body wants to take the path of least resistance; it always wants to go the easy way. However, it takes discipline to push through to get the results you want, and it all starts with your words.

You can confess yourself out of your bondage. The Bible says that sin has no more dominion over you. Someone may say, *"Once a drug addict, always a drug addict,"* or *"Once an alcoholic, always an alcoholic."* I beg your pardon; that is not a confession that should be coming out of anyone's mouth. If you have been in these situations, your confession should be, *"I once was an alcoholic, but I am absolutely NOT anymore."* You must speak your way out of bondage. You cannot break the power of pornography over your life if you don't believe you can.

What's Your confession?

Is your confession, *"I can't seem to control alcohol, drugs, pornography, etc.,"* or is it, *"Sin has no dominion over me"*? I'm not a nervous wreck; I am calm as a cucumber. What are you going to let come from your mouth? You are the controlling witness. Are you going to let the devil knock you around for the rest of your life, or will you stand up and do something about it? Jesus is coming; we must get it under control!

"Well, I can't get control of these credit cards." It is not your credit cards you need to control; it is your mouth. Credit cards are a secondary issue. The power for your life is in your tongue. Are you going to do anything about it, or will you gripe about it and contact the prayer line? You can call the prayer line till the cows come home, however long that is, but you must take control of your tongue.

My question to you is: When are you going to do something about it? You are the determining witness of your life concerning what is going to happen with your future.

We are not just exercising mind over matter; we employ our minds over our bodies. You must understand how to do this. If you can bridle your tongue, you can bridle the body because the tongue sets on fire the course of your future. This strategy is how you get bound by something. The devil and all of hell are shooting at your tongue. He wants to gain control of your tongue so he can create a faulty confession from your mouth and get you accustomed to saying it. He wants you to say it until you believe it and then act on it until it perpetuates in your life.

Long Lasting Benefits

A person might say, *"I hate going to the gym. I know I ought to work out, but I just can't seem to do it."* Do you know what my confession is? *"I love to go to the gym. I enjoy it. That is one of my favorite things to do."* It really is; I am not just saying that. However, I will say that when I started saying it, it was not my favorite thing to do. Now, it's like my escape valve or safety net; it's fun for me. The fountain of youth is not in a bottle; it's in the gym.

I saw an interview the other day with a sixty-one-year-old guy. When he was playing college football, he was an excellent athlete and would have probably gone pro. At the end of his sophomore year, this guy got into trouble and was kicked off the team. It broke his heart, but he still loved football. So, he got a job as a strength coach. The team he was dismissed from had a reunion, and some teammates were talking to him about what had happened. He spoke of his many regrets and his love for the game. They suggested he try out for his old college team because he still had two years of eligibility. Remember, he is sixty-one years old! He tried out, made the team, and played well. They asked him, "What's the number one factor in your ability to make the team?" His answer: strength training.

Here's a man of 61 who is able to compete at a level that men forty years his junior were doing. However, you cannot get your body under control like he did unless you get your mouth under control first. It's supernatural. God will begin to help you if you first apply His laws and principles to your life.

If you always talk about what you can't do, how you will never make it, or how it's all going to fall apart, God will not help you. You must get your tongue under control first, and then these other things will begin to follow.

"Well, I'm just a hopeless addict," you say. No, you are not hopeless. You may have been an addict, but you can break this thing with the power of your words. God is showing you how to get control of your life by using your words.

Meditate and Act

This word "meditate," which we saw in Joshua 1:8 at the beginning of this chapter, means to say something over and over. If you meditate on the Word, you are repeatedly saying the words or the verses to yourself. Notice how this verse is worded: after you meditate on the Word, "...then **thou** shalt make thy way prosperous..." It does not say that God will make your way prosperous. Instead, as you begin to talk right and speak the Word, this verse says God is going to give you ideas; He's going to give you witty inventions; He's going to give you a mechanism to show you what to do and how to go about it.

We tend to say something once and expect God to blast into our living room, pick us off the sofa, and make us do something. He is not going to do that; He is going to show you what to do. He will show you the means to fix your situation, and He will help you do it, but He will not do it for you.

The rest of Joshua 1:8 reads, "...then thou shalt make thy way prosperous, and then thou shalt have good success." It does not say that God is going to make you a success. God told Joshua if he would meditate on the Word day and night, he would have prosperity and good success.

> "Let the words of my mouth, and the meditation of
> my heart, be acceptable in thy sight, O Lord, my
> strength, and my redeemer" (Psalm 19:14).

God is saying that the meditations of your heart will go together with the words you speak. You will not say what you don't meditate on first. If you think wrongly, you are going to say wrong things.

This psalm is saying: Let everything I think and all that goes on in my mind be pleasing to You. We often get concerned about our actions when we are trying to discipline our lives and trying to do the "Christian thing"—*"I can't do this; I should do that; I don't do this; I must do that"*—but change starts with what you think about before you ever get to your actions. God is bringing it to a whole different level. He is talking about what goes on **in you** before any actions take place.

I pray this verse for myself quite often. I say, *"Lord, I don't just want what I do externally to be pleasing to you. Of course, I want that, but I want my external actions to be quality actions—Christian actions—godly actions—the right kind of actions."* God knows it is much more than that because He said let the words of your mouth and the meditations of your heart be acceptable in His sight. If the meditations of your heart are right and the words of your mouth are right, then the actions will follow suit. Your actions are the natural result of your thoughts.

The power of speaking faith-filled words is critical to each of us. You cannot talk poverty and still live in God's blessing. You cannot talk stupidity and have the mind of Christ. You cannot talk about your weariness and have energy. You cannot talk your failures and have success. You cannot often speak of your "I cant's" and be an "I can." You must say it before you see it.

God will begin to bring what you say to pass, even if it is one small step at a time. Some things will be quicker than others, but even if it is little by little, you cannot talk your sicknesses and have God's healing. You cannot talk about what you cannot do and move to the next level. You must speak the favor of God on your life. You must talk about your capabilities in God:

> *I can do all things through Christ, which strengthens me. The Greater One lives in me. I don't see any way to do this, Lord, but You know how to do it. Since You live in me, I'm going to say that I'm a world overcomer. I'm going to say that You meet my needs according to Your riches in glory. I don't see any other way for that to happen.*

My Journey

When I was a young man, thinking about and visualizing the future ahead of me, I would see something and think, *"Wouldn't that be nice if someday I could live in that, or have that, or enjoy that?"* I'm not talking about greed; I'm talking about the dreams that make up life. From the bottom of a grateful heart, God has given me all the things I dreamt about as a young man, plus some.

I have never believed I was poor. I have never believed I was incapable. Someone may think I am incapable, but they just don't know enough yet. You haven't seen me in action. There's just a determination in me that won't allow someone else to hang that on me because it doesn't fit here, and there is nothing external to prove it.

Nothing.

When you've lived long enough to look back and reflect on it, you can see that it was the Lord inspiring you. He put you in a position to see something you've never seen and gave you a desire for it.

When Nora and I first married, I had just left the military, and neither of us had a job. Thank God for good parents. One positive thing about it was we didn't have any debt either. We were just kids starting out; she was eighteen, and I was twenty. When you have a clean slate, you can write it any way you want. But we have never—our whole married life—never believed there was anything we couldn't do. At that age, you're too stupid to know you're stupid —just two kids with dreams, faith in God, and knowledge of these principles.

149

How to Change the World

Let me leave you with this: God is not just on the talking side of things; He is also into the acting side. Action must be put with your faith confessions. You release faith in two ways: by saying and by doing. You can have all the faith in you that God could ever grant, plus all you could muster up, but if you don't say it and you don't do it, it will never change anything.

Faith in your heart will not change anything. It's faith in your heart and in your mouth, coupled with your actions, that will change the world.

ABOUT THE AUTHOR

DR. ED KING is the founder and Senior Pastor of Redemption Church in Knoxville, Tennessee. He also serves as the president of "The Power of the Word" television ministry, which broadcasts to both national and international markets. In addition to these duties, Dr. King has authored nine books to date and traveled to over 60 nations around the world—teaching and preaching the gospel to thousands of people in leadership conferences and evangelistic meetings. He makes his home in Knoxville with his wife and co-Pastor, Nora King. Together they have a daughter, Laren, and son, Marcus, who is in heaven.

Power of the Word Ministries
Dr. Ed King
PO Box 52466
Knoxville TN 37950 USA
1.800.956.4433
www.poweroftheword.com
info@poweroftheword.com
youtube.com/user/RedemptionChurch

Redemption Church
3550 Pleasant Ridge Rd
Knoxville TN 37921 USA
865.521.7777
www.redemptionchurch.com
info@redemptionchurch.com
youtube.com/user/RedemptionChurch

BOOKS BY DR. ED KING

WILL MY PET BE IN HEAVEN?
ISBN: 9781602730687 • 92 pages.

COOPERATING WITH YOUR DESTINY
ISBN: 9781602731349 • 232 pages.

LOYALTY—Going Beyond Faithfulness
ISBN: 9781602730793 • 110 pages.

THE TIMING OF GOD—His Timetable for Your Life
ISBN: 978160273717 • 118 pages.

DEDICATING YOUR HOUSE
ISBN: 9781602730861 • 114 pages.

WHAT'S GOING ON?
Why I Believe We Are the Rapture Generation
ISBN: 9781973638872 • 298 pages • Westbow Press

BOOKS BY DR. ED KING

COOPERATING WITH YOUR DESTINY—Discovering God's Plan for Your Life

Seeking God's purpose for your life—what He put you on this planet to do—is the most important thing you could ever pursue! God has a good plan for your life that has been designed just for you. Your destiny is a partnership with God orchestrated to cause you to flourish and obtain your eternal reward—all you have to do is join with God's plan!
ISBN: 9781602731349 • 232 pages • Parsons Publishing House

DEDICATING YOUR HOUSE

Dedicating your house is a rite that every Christian should perform in order to live a quiet and peaceful life. Because you live in your house, you should want and expect God's blessings on it. One way to see those blessings is to thoughtfully and sacredly separate your house for the Lord's work and service. In this book, Dr. King lays out the biblical case for dedicating your house and provides eight easy-to-follow steps.
ISBN: 9781602730861 • 114 pages • Parsons Publishing House

THE TIMING OF GOD—His Timetable for Your Life

In this life–changing book, you will discover the true timetable that God has set up for you at creation. You will see everything in life has a time and a season. God wants to give you remarkable things to experience, but He wants to give them to you when you are ready to handle and enjoy them. After reading and studying this book, you will become more assured than ever that your next move will be by the inspiration and the timing of God.
ISBN: 978160273717 • 118 pages • Parsons Publishing House

BOOKS BY DR. ED KING

SPEAKING FAITH-FILLED Words—How Words Shape Your World

Everyone wants to enjoy life and be satisfied! Having a good life is not about wealth or entitlement but about connecting with God, operating in faith, and living in His promises. Veteran author, Dr. Ed King, tells you how to embrace God's promises through speaking faith-filled words. It's time to engage God with your burning faith and release your words to shape your world
ISBN: 9781602731486 • 160 pages • Parsons Publishing House

LOYALTY—Going Beyond Faithfulness

Pastor Ed King elaborates on the distinctions between faithfulness and loyalty and focuses on lessons learned by looking at the brotherly love of Jonathan and David. Learn how God's grace will meet you to go past faithfulness and enter into loyalty. It all starts with a decision!
ISBN: 9781602730793 • 110 pages • Parsons Publishing House

WILL MY PET BE IN HEAVEN?

In this book, Pastor Ed King gives us a solid, biblical answer about your pet's afterlife. If you or someone you know has lost a pet, you will find great comfort and insight into what the Bible has to say about our beloved animals and their future in heaven.
ISBN: 9781602730687 • 92 pages • Parsons Publishing House

WHAT'S GOING ON?—Why I Believe We Are the Rapture Generation

Although the Bible tells us that no one knows the day or the hour of Jesus' return, God's Word does reveal solid information that illustrates how the signs of the times are lining up for His return to the earth. Pastor Ed King shares insight about the many signs appearing and circumstances playing out at this very hour.
ISBN: 9781973638872 • 298 pages • Westbow Press

BOOKS BY NORA KING

OVERCOMING IN DIFFICULT TIMES

Based on her own experiences and biblical insight, Nora King shares practical ways to rise above the ashes of difficulty and despair. You can move from tragedy to triumph. Don't give up; rise up and live again!

ISBN: 9781602731189
152 pages

30 DAYS TO A BETTER PRAYER LIFE

In this exciting book, Nora King offers fresh revelation and practical teaching to help you experience the release of God's power. You will learn daily how to improve your prayer life and enter God's presence through these simple principles. You don't have to struggle to pray any longer!

ISBN: 9781602730120
142 pages

Parsons Publishing House
Your Voice Your World ™

Available at your local or online bookstores and www.redemptionchurch.com.